BEYOND JENNIFER AND JASON

AN ENLIGHTENED GUIDE TO NAMING YOUR BABY

• • • • • • • • • • • •

LINDA ROSENKRANTZ
& PAMELA REDMOND SATRAN

St. Martin's Press
New York

BEYOND JENNIFER AND JASON. Copyright © 1988, 1990 by Linda Rosenkrantz and Pamela Redmond Satran. All rights reserved. Printed in the United States of America. No part of this book may be used or reproduced in any manner whatsoever without written permission except in the case of brief quotations embodied in critical articles or reviews. For information, address St. Martin's Press, 175 Fifth Avenue, New York, N.Y. 10010.

Library of Congress Cataloging-in-Publication Data

Rosenkrantz, Linda.
    Beyond Jennifer and Jason : an enlightened guide to naming your
baby / Linda Rosenkrantz and Pamela Redmond Satran. — [Rev. and
updated ed.]
        p.   cm.
    ISBN 0-312-05384-3
    1. Names, Personal—United States.   I. Satran, Pamela
Redmond.   II. Title.
CS2377.R67   1991
929.4′4′0973—dc20

90-19118
CIP

10 9 8 7 6 5 4 3 2 1

For our wonderful daughters
Chloe Samantha Finch
and
Rory Elizabeth Margaret Satran

CONTENTS

ACKNOWLEDGMENTS

Our first thanks go to our editor, Hope Dellon, for believing in this project and for bringing it to its perfect realization. Also, we want to thank our agent, Howard Morhaim, for his energy and enthusiasm. And special thanks to Nancy Fish for her early input and Joseph Redmond for his early encouragement; to Fred Krantz of the Wisconsin Department of Health and Social Services for his tremendous guidance in compiling statistics on most-popular names; to Roger Smith of the California Health Demographics Section and Tim Smith of the New York State Health Department for their help on popularity rankings; to Rabbi Mark Hurvitz for advice on Jewish naming traditions and Hebrew names; to Emily Shapiro for her help with Creative Class; to Rita DiMatteo for insights into Italian-American naming traditions; to Alison Acker, for her helpful suggestions; to the parents whose real-life considerations when naming their children provided inspiration for this book—Andrea and Alan Higbie, Marian Golan, Peter Richmond and Melissa Davis, Mary Jo Kochakian, Chuck and Jone Fulkerson, and Mary Jean Shalhoub; and finally thanks to our husbands, Christopher Finch and Richard Satran, for understanding the obsession.

INTRODUCTION

The first, most important, and most lasting gift you bestow on your baby is a name. The aim of this book is to lead you to the perfect choice for your child, a name with which your son or daughter can live happily ever after.

Most other name books consist of one long alphabetical list; *Beyond Jennifer and Jason* offers almost a hundred separate lists, designed both to awaken you to new possibilities and to narrow the focus of your own personal slate of candidates. Where other books tell you that Cameron means "crooked nose" in Scotch Gaelic and Rachel means "a female sheep" in Hebrew, this book deals with contemporary perceptions of these names in the preschool and the playground and beyond. Here you will find lists devoted to trendy names, fashionable names and names due for a revival, lists of names that project brains and those that project beauty, lists of boyish names for girls and macho names for boys, some surprising names of saints and names that follow the "kosher curve." In other words, you will find lists to guide

you through every concern, satisfy every naming consideration you may have.

And we don't just abandon you to the list; each is sup-
ported by pertinent information: How kids feel about having
the same name as four of their friends, for instance, or what
psychologists say about the effect of offbeat names. Which
ambisexual names are becoming too girlish for boys, and what
you should keep in mind about nicknames, middle names,
and sibling names. What it's like for a boy to be a junior,
and why you should think twice about naming your child
after someone famous.

All the information you need to make an informed and
felicitous choice is organized into four easy-to-follow sections:

Style: A look at popularity, fashion, and trends. Here's where
you'll find details on which names are in, out, hot, not. Fresh
names for the nineties. Also here: the only accurate list of
most-popular names, the only comprehensive guide to what
the rich, famous, and royal are naming their children.

Image: A guide to the impressions names project. In this section you'll find names with the power to evoke brains, creativity, energy, and beauty. Names with newfound class,
names that will help your child both fit in and stand out,
and names that may prove too much—or not enough—for
your little one to live up to.

Sex: Signposts for negotiating the gender maze. Girls' names
are divided into four groups, from ultrafeminine to boyish.
Boys' names are categorized from macho to wimpy. And the
ever widening pool of ambisexual names is organized for you
from the most girlish to the almost exclusively male.

Tradition: A look at the history, the ethnic and religious meanings of names. Names that reflect your unique background, including hundreds of surprising and unusual choices. Also here: How to find a name you and your spouse both love (and why you may have trouble doing so); choosing a name with baby's brothers and sisters—existing or future—in mind.

A note on the spelling of names in this book: For the most part, we have used only the most classic spelling of each name. When more than one variation is listed (Catherine/ Katherine, for example), it is because both spellings are equally proper and well-accepted.

It's possible to use this book for consultation on names you already know you like: to find out, for instance, whether Emily is considered classic or trendy, whether Whitney still has any masculine punch. Or you can start with the qualities most important to you and use this book to find names that satisfy them: to cull a list of selections that work for either a boy or girl, that sound energetic, that aren't too trendy, and that have Celtic roots, for example. We think the best way to read this book is as a whole, using a combination of the two techniques. When you find a category that appeals— Creative Power Names, say—choose specific examples you like and then check the index for other sections in which they appear.

And in the end, you'll have the pleasure of knowing you have made a thoughtful and enlightened choice, whether you decide to move beyond Jennifer and Jason or not.

STYLE

▼

What do we mean by style in terms of naming your baby?

Ideally, we're talking about personal style: finding a name that reflects your taste, that moves beyond fad and fashion, yet succeeds in catching the sound and spirit of the age.

Your attitudes towards style in other aspects of your life—from clothing and furniture to the way you live and your vision of the world—will affect your judgments about style in names. Whether you're conservative or liberal, care about being in fashion or rebel against it, set trends or avoid them, will all influence the style of the name you choose.

Because style changes constantly, differentiating among the names that are trendy and those that are fashionable, the names that are due for a comeback and those that are hopelessly out of date, can be difficult. That's where this section can act as your guide.

First, we outline current style: the names being used by fashionable people right now. Many of these names may not be widely popular this year, but they're heading there.

Next, you'll find a comprehensive list of the names that have been topping popularity lists for the past few years. These are the trendy names, threatened by overexposure, that you may find so far in they're out. If some of your favorites appear on this list, take heart: We also offer a selection of fresher-sounding substitutes for Jennifer, Jason, and friends.

If your desire is to find a name in the vanguard of style, the lists for you are those in the chapter of names that are so far out they're in. These are the names we believe will set the fashions for the next decade and beyond.

And if you want to find a name that truly bucks fashion— or if you want to avoid the names that are hopelessly out of style—consult the list of names that are so far out they'll always be out.

You may want to compare the names you like with those the rest of the world is choosing. Here you'll find lists of the most popular names in the United States, as well as a comprehensive catalog of what the rich, famous, and royal have been naming their children. The celebrity section also includes names linked to real people and fictional characters— names as accessible as Ally, as off-limits as Oprah—and why you should think twice about letting a star's popularity be your naming guide.

WHAT'S HOT

The major naming trends of today have one thing in common: They're all tied to tradition. Cute names, made-up names, five-minute fads, and other flights of fancy are out. Names that sound as if they've been plucked from the family tree are in.

We've divided the currently stylish names into three categories: Restored Classics, Grandma and Grandpa, and Androgynous Executive. You won't find most of the names here on any popularity lists. Some are still on the cutting edge of style; some are just beginning to have wider appeal. And many of these names will probably remain precisely what they are now: fashionable, but not commonplace.

But other names here—notably several on the Grandma and Grandpa list—are already joining the ranks of names that are so far in they're out. That's the danger in giving your child a fashionable name: However fresh, attractive, "right" it sounds today, it could seem all too popular a few years down the road. If your main intention is to choose a name no one else is choosing, be warned. You might be picking a Jennifer of Jason of the future.

RESTORED CLASSIC NAMES

The names we call Restored Classics can be likened to the grand old houses that were neglected a generation ago, the Colonials and Victorians passed over in favor of spiffier ranches or split-levels, or geodesic domes. So too were these traditional names left to molder while newly constructed names like Cheryl and Gary and even Leaf were choice properties.

But today, just as young parents are pulling up the shag carpets and sanding the wood floors in their new old houses, so too are they reviving classic names—good solid names—that have been around for centuries. Where once these names were seen as outmoded hulks, now they're considered the epitome of good taste.

The conservative tone of the eighties did much to restore traditional names to favor. The first wave of classics to be revived—names we called Nouveau Conservatif in the 1988 edition of this book—were standards such as Jane and Katherine, William and Henry. It was no coincidence that William and Henry were also the names chosen by Prince Charles and Princess Diana for their eighties sons.

And then along came Fergie, who pushed the trend further by choosing for her two little princesses born on the cusp of the nineties names plucked from our original Baby Men and Women list: Beatrice and Eugenie. In fact, in the wake of Beatrice and Eugenie, several names are jumping from that avant-garde list to this one, giving the group a fresh twist along with a new title. Of the hot names detailed in this section, these new Restored Classics are unequivocally the hottest.

If you choose a name from the Restored Classics list, rest assured that no one will ever call you a slave to fashion. But just because these names have been used for ages does not mean they transcend trendiness. Rather, they're part of a trend to ignore what's trendy, to be different from everyone who's trying to be different. If parents continue in this naming direction at the same clip, we'll greet the new millennium with an awful lot of baby Olivias and Fredericks in tow.

Restored classic names

G I R L S

ALICE	HELEN
ANNE	HOPE
BEATRICE	ISABEL
CAROLINE	JANE
CATHERINE/	JOSEPHINE
KATHERINE	JULIA
CELIA	LOUISE
CHARLOTTE	LUCY
CLAIRE	MADEL(E)INE
EDITH	MARGARET
ELEANOR	MARTHA
ELIZABETH	NATALIE
EVE	NORA
GRACE	OLIVIA

PHOEBE
ROSE
SALLY

SOPHIA
VIRGINIA

B O Y S

ANDREW
CHARLES
DANIEL
DAVID
EDWARD
FREDERICK
GEORGE
HENRY
HUGH
JAMES

JOHN
JOSEPH
PATRICK
PAUL
PETER
PHIL(L)IP
ROBERT
THOMAS
WILLIAM

GRANDMA AND GRANDPA NAMES

Grandma and Grandpa names are not pretty names. They are earthy as opposed to glossy, plain as opposed to fancy, humble as opposed to pretentious. In these ways they go as far beyond Jennifer and Jason as you can get.

Grandma and Grandpa names celebrate the beauty of the *hamish*, the unadorned, the ordinary. Theirs is the style of unfinished pine furniture, rag rugs, and hand-stitched quilts. There's a certain hipness in their rejection of all that glitters, as there is in a movie star who lives on a ranch instead of in Hollywood. These names don't try too hard; they don't really try at all. And therein lies the secret of their charm.

You will notice that several of the names on the Grandma

and Grandpa list are nicknames. Many people are simply bestowing these familiar forms on their children—just plain Sam or Lizzie or Maggie. But others will choose a proper name—Samuel or Elizabeth or Margaret—for the sole purpose of getting the Grandma and Grandpa nickname. The advantage of going with the proper name, of course, is that if your little Lizzie grows up and decides she wants to be a commodities broker rather than a weaver, she has the option of calling herself Elizabeth. And although that time seems a long way off, Elizabeth will look more impressive than Lizzie on a job application.

If you choose a Grandma or Grandpa name for your child, you are probably looking for something out of the ordinary, a name that may never sound attractive enough to be trendy. Some parents of Sams and Maxes have told us they liked the names because they were too downright homely to be chosen by very many other people. Well, we have news for them. Just as Robert Redford, Sissy Spacek, and Jessica Lange have rejected Hollywood glamour and pretense by retreating to remote farms and ranches, so too are there lots of little Sams and Maxes ambling into the world. As one sad parent of a five-year-old Max put it: "Max isn't Max anymore. Now, if you want to name your kid Max, you've got to name him Gus."

Grandma and Grandpa names

G I R L S

ANNA	BESS
ANNIE	CEIL
BECKY	EMMA

FANNY	MAGGIE
GOLDIE	MOLLY
HANNAH	NELL
JENNY	ROSIE
JESSIE	SADIE
KATE	SARA(H)
LEAH	SONIA
LIBBY	SOPHIE
LILY	TESS
LIZZIE	WILLA

B O Y S

ABE	HARRY
BEN	JACK
CAL	JAKE
CHARLIE	JOE
CLEM	MAX
ELI	NAT
FRANK	NED
FRED	SAM
GUS	WILL

ANDROGYNOUS EXECUTIVE NAMES

Is it a boy? Is it a girl? Is it a future CEO? Nursery schools, colleges, and corporations will one day be wondering, but only the parents will know for sure.

Names we classify as Androgynous Executive—names sometimes used by preppies and Southerners in the past— were fostered by the feminist movement and promoted further by the corporate, competitive eighties. The current style is to use most of these names for girls rather than boys, as it is still considered more of an advantage for a girl to possess masculine qualities than for a boy to embody feminine ones. Of course, some of these names—Gordon, Reed, Cameron— have retained a distinctly masculine bent, and are still used mostly for boys. But others, such as Whitney, Page, and Ashley, are now thoroughly feminized, so their androgynous advantage—if you choose to see it as that—is fading.

For the most part, however, these are not boys' names or girls' names—they are surnames, patrician-sounding enough to confer upon a child an automatic pedigree. Whether you can really claim a Whitney or a Morgan as an ancestor doesn't matter: The objective is a well-bred image. Image is what sets these names apart from other ambisexual names like Casey or Jody. Giving a girl an Androgynous Executive name doesn't say you want her to be a cute little tomboy, but rather that you are looking ahead to her capable, forceful womanhood. For a boy, the image is slightly different: Yes, he's from the kind of family that could foot the bill for Harvard Business School if that's where he wanted to go, but he might just as easily choose to be a painter instead.

Examine the various branches of your own family tree. Great-grandma's maiden name or an uncle's middle name, hidden away on the pages of an old photograph album or family Bible, might make an original yet authentic first-name choice for your son or daughter.

Androgynous executive names

ABBOTT
ADDISON
AMORY
ARCHER
ARDEN
AVERELL
AVERY
BLAINE
BLAIR
BLAKE
BROOKS
BROWN
CAMERON
CARSON
CARTER
FARRELL
GORDON
HARPER
JORDAN
KEIL
KENDALL
KENYON
KIMBALL
KIRBY
KYLE
LANE
MACKENZIE
MALLORY
MORGAN
NORRIS
PA(I)GE
PALMER
PARKER
PAXTON
PEYTON
PORTER
PRICE
REED
SCHUYLER
SLOAN
TAYLOR
WALKER

Why Jordan and Taylor Will Never Be Hot Names in Norway

According to Norwegian Name Law, Paragraph 15, Number 2 (no, we're not kidding), parents are forbidden from giving their children names "that are or have been used as surnames and are not originally first names." Among those names prohibited: Russell, as in Bertrand, and Scott, as in Sir Walter.

Surname-names are permitted for use as middle names, provided they carry some genuine family connection. The mother's maiden name is okay; so is the earlier surname of an adopted child. But if parents want to give their child a surname-middle name with less evident family ties, they have to prove to the government that the name has "special affiliation through the family or some other way." Just thinking it's cute, in other words, is not reason enough.

The Norwegian Name Law also forbids any name that is "a disadvantage to whom it is given." Examples cited: Adolph and Elvis.

So Far in They're Out

The whole issue of trendiness in names is a double-edged sword. For the most part, kids like having popular names; they like swimming in the mainstream. You wouldn't find many seven-year-old Samanthas, Seans, or Sams out there who would say they hated their names. On the other hand, there might be quite a few twenty-seven-year-old Sharis, Scotts, or Shelleys who would voice some regrets at being known to the world by those epidemic names of the sixties.

We present the following master list of So Far In They're Out names so that if you choose one of them for your child, it will be with the knowledge that these names carry with them this dilemma of trendiness. Even if there aren't any Brandons or Caitlins or Jesses on your block yet, it doesn't mean they aren't trendy names. As fresh as some of them may sound to your ear, there's a good chance that three other kids with the same name will be in your child's kindergarten class.

But what if Nicole is your favorite name despite its trendy

status? Either forge ahead with it, knowing that your Nicole will bring something unique to the name, or consult the substitution guide that follows.

So far in they're out names

G I R L S

ALEXANDRA	DANA
ALEXIS	DANIELLE
AL(L)ISON	DAWN
ALYSSA (and	ERICA
variations like	ERIN
ILISSA, ELICIA,	HAYLEY/HALEY
et al)	HEATHER
AMANDA	HIL(L)ARY
AMBER	JAMIE
AMY	JENNIFER
ANNIE	JENNY
ARIEL	JESSICA
ASHLEY	JESSIE
BETHANY	JORDAN
BRITTANY	KAYLA
BROOKE	KELLY
CAITLIN	KIM
CHELSEA	KIMBERLY
CHRISSIE	KIRSTEN
CHRISTIE	KRISTIN
CHRISTINA	LAUREN
COURTNEY	LINDSAY/LINDSEY
CRYSTAL	LISA

MEGAN

MELANIE

MELISSA

MICHELLE

MOLLY

NICOLE

RACHEL

SABRINA

SAMANTHA

SHANNON

STEPHANIE

TARA

TIFFANY

TRACY

VANESSA

WHITNEY

B O Y S

AARON

ADAM

ALEX

ALEXANDER

ASHLEY

BEN

BENJAMIN

BLAKE

BRADLEY

BRANDON

BRENDAN

BRETT

BRIAN

CASEY

CODY

DARRYL

DUSTIN

DYLAN

ERIC

ETHAN

IAN

JACOB

JAKE

JAMIE

JASON

JEREMY

JESSE

JONATHAN

JORDAN

JOSHUA

JUSTIN

KEVIN

KYLE

LOREN

LUKE

MATTHEW

MAX

NICHOLAS

RYAN

SAM

SAMUEL

SCOTT

SEAN   TYLER
TIMOTHY   ZACHARY
TODD   ZACK
TRAVIS

FASHIONABLE CLASSICS

Fashionable classics are names that, while they happen to be
trendy right now, nonetheless have staying power. If you give
your child one of these fashionable classic names, you should
know that he or she will be one of many with the same name.
Nevertheless, these names won't necessarily brand him forever as a child of the nineties, the way their faddier cousins—
Joshua, Jessica, et al—might.

Some of the following are among the most widely used
names on the Restored Classics list; others figure promi-
nently on most-popular lists around the country. What we
consider fashionable classics for girls are:

ANNE   KATE
CAROLINE   KATHERINE (this is
CHRISTINE   the fashionable
ELIZABETH   spelling)
EMILY   LAURA
JANE   LUCY
JULIA   SARA(H)

For boys, the fashionable classics are:

ANDREW   CHRISTOPHER
CHARLES   DANIEL

DAVID	NICHOLAS
EDWARD	PETER
HENRY	STEPHEN
JAMES	THOMAS
JOHN	TIMOTHY
MATTHEW	WILLIAM
MICHAEL	

BUT NICOLE IS MY FAVORITE NAME!

If all the foregoing has depressed you, if you've wanted to name your daughter Nicole since you were twelve years old and were not aware that thousands of other people had the same idea, we offer in apology a selection of names you might consider substituting for too-trendy favorites. What you consider an overused name or an acceptable substitute is to some extent a matter of personal style. Not all of the names on the "instead of" list have been pegged as so far in they're out, and some of the substitutes make a big leap forward in fashion. However, all of the possible substitute names bear some relationship to their overexposed counterparts in sound, feel, or taste, but their color is brighter and their texture a bit crisper.

G I R L S

Instead of:	Consider:
ALEXANDRA	ARABELLA
AL(L)ISON	ALICE
ALYSSA	ELIZA
AMANDA	MIRANDA
ASHLEY	AVERY

CAITLIN	KATHLEEN or BRONWEN
COURTNEY	SYDNEY
DANA	DINAH
DANIELLE	LUCIENNE or SIMONE
EMILY	EMMA or EMILIA
ERIN	DEVON
HAYLEY/HALEY	LEILA or HIL(L)ARY
HEATHER	ROSEMARY or LILY
JENNIFER	JENNA
JESSICA	JESSA or JESSAMINE
JESSIE	JOSIE
JORDAN	GEORGIA
KELLY	KELSEY or QUINN
KIMBERLY	KIRBY or CHLOE
KRISTIN	KRISTA/CHRISTA
LAUREN	LAUREL
LINDSAY/LINDSEY	LACEY
LISA	LIZA or LUCY
MEGAN	REGAN or MARGARET
MELISSA	PRISCILLA or LARISSA
MOLLY	POLLY or DAISY

NICOLE	NICOLA
RACHEL	LEAH or RAYNA
SAMANTHA	SUSANNAH or SOPHIA
SHANNON	SHEA
TARA	NORA
TIFFANY	TESSA
TRACY	GRACE
VANESSA	VIOLET or CASSANDRA

B O Y S

Instead of:	Consider:
AARON	ABNER or EZRA
ADAM	AIDAN
ALEX	ALEC
BRANDON	BRAM
BRETT	BRICE
BRIAN	BRENNAN
CASEY	CLAY or CLANCY
CHRISTOPHER	CHRISTIAN
DYLAN	DUNCAN
ERIC	EMMETT
GARY	GRAY
JACOB	CALEB
JAKE	ABE or JACK
JASON	JASPER
JEREMY	JEREMIAH

JONATHAN	JONAS or JOHN
JORDAN	GEORGE
JOSHUA	JOSIAH
JUSTIN	JULIAN
KEVIN	CALVIN
MATTHEW	MATTHIAS
MAX	HARRY
NICHOLAS	TREVOR or COLIN
RYAN	RILEY
SAM	GUS or SIMM
SAMUEL	SAMSON
SEAN	SHAW
ZACHARY	ZACHARIAH
ZACK	ZEKE

So far out they're on their way in

As the good ships Jennifer and Jason, Adam and Amy sail slowly out to sea for a well-deserved respite, what new fleet of names will begin to drift in? We foresee certain trends continuing, certain substitutions taking place, other old sources being tapped, different historical periods coming up for reconsideration.

Heaven knows the babies of today and tomorrow are entering a difficult and dangerous world, and there are two polar approaches you can take to meet this reality: arm or disarm. In the armed camp is a battalion of no-nonsense, no-nickname, responsible, bankable, grown-up citizen names. On the other side are the jaunty names: a raft of casual, happy-go-lucky, nothing-dire-can-befall-someone-with-such-a-cheery-name names.

Following is our selection of pick-hit names from both camps. These are names for the nineties and beyond, names that have style but aren't trendy, that sound new but not invented, that are solid but not blah.

THE O-NAMES

Friendliest of the whole crop of names that are so far out they're in are the names—primarily for boys—that end with the letter O. They almost seem to grin and call out a disarming "Hello!" We've already heard a few trend-setting tykes with o-ending nicknames: a Benjamin who's called Benno and a Charles who was immediately dubbed Carlo. Some o-named grown-ups already in the mainstream are Arsenio Hall, Emilio Estevez, Marlo Thomas, and Benno Schmidt, president of Yale University; also having an influence is Theo, the teenaged Cosby Show character.

Despite their breeziness, these names are not lightweight. The final *o* connotes a measure of strength we don't find in other vowel-ending names, such as Jessa or Jody.

There are a few good o-names for girls: Cleo, Lilo, Margo, Caro, and Marlo. For boys, the most likely to succeed of these spirited ultimate-o names are:

ALDO	LORENZO
ALONZO	MARCO
ARLO	MILO
ARNO	NICO
BENNO	ORLANDO
BRUNO	OTTO
COSMO	PHILO
ELMO	ROCCO
EMILIO	ROLLO
HORATIO	THEO
HUGO	VITO
JETHRO	WALDO
LEO	

Viva Leo!

His real name was Leonard, Len. He'd changed it when he came East. "Len," he said. "A turd of a name. Who wants it? I mean, a name that ends in a nasalization, for Christ's sake. Leo, now. It's like Anna. They go on forever. You can *live* with a name like that."

—Sue Miller, *The Good Mother*

THE RAF PILOT NAMES

Sharing an air of jaunty confidence with the O-names is a group of white-silk-scarved RAF Pilot names not yet in wide use in this country but poised for an imminent landing. They're on the cutting edge of fashion, combining the style of upper-crust England with the élan of the leather bomber jacket. We'd put them in the armed camp if they weren't so charming: You just know they will land their planes in time for tea. Fight the urge to give your son a little cowboy name and consider instead:

ADRIAN	COLIN
ALISTAIR	DAMIEN
BASIL	DEREK
CLIVE	DESMOND
CRISPIN	DUNCAN

GILES	MILES
GRAHAM	NIGEL
GUY	NOEL
HUGH	REX
IVOR	ROBIN
JULIAN	RUPERT
LIONEL	SEBASTIAN
MALCOLM	TREVOR

Nigel happens to be one of the names I've been crusading for as part of a plan to further Anglo-American friendship. I've always thought that one reason the English resent Americans is that we've never been able to favor the boys' names they favor, and they've always suspected us of thinking that their names are for sissies. Now here's my plan: For the next few years, a lot of Americans name their boys Nigel and Cecil and Cyril and Trevor and Simon, and we invite the English to name their boys American names. . . . Then, sooner or later, the United States will have a lot of grown-up men with English-sounding names and there will be a lot of people in England named LeRoy and Sonny and Bubba.

—Calvin Trillin, *Newsday*

THE IRISH SURNAME NAMES

From the days of "Sweet Rosie O'Grady" and "I'll Take You Home Again, Kathleen," Irish names have been consistently popular in this country. In the seventies and early eighties, Erin and Kelly and Shannon were among the top fifty names for girls, while Brian, Ryan, and Sean were equally popular boys' names.

Now, for the first time, we see an invasion of Irish surnames-as-first-names approaching. These Irish immigrants are claiming land pioneered by their now-established blue-blood counterparts—Morgan, Whitney, Ashley, Porter, and relatives—and infusing the last-names-first breed with fresh blood and new vigor.

While many of these names have long been used in Ireland for boys, in America most will work as well for girls. If this kind of name appeals to you, tap your own Irish roots for a family name, or look to this list:

BLAINE	CULLEN
BOWIE	CURRAN
BRADY	DEMPSEY
BRENNAN	DESMOND
BRODY	DEVLIN
CAGNEY	DOLAN
CALHOUN	DONAHUE
CALLAHAN	DONNELLY
CASSIDY	DONOVAN
CLANCY	DUNHAM
CONARY	EGAN
CONNELL	FALLON
CONROY	FARRELL

FINN	MAGILL
FINNIAN	NOLAN
FLANAGAN	PHELAN
FLANNERY	QUINLAN
FLYNN	QUINN
GANNON	REDMOND
GRADY	REGAN
GRIFFIN	RILEY
HOGAN	SHAW
KANE	SHEA
KEARNEY	SHERIDAN
KEENAN	SWEENEY
KENNEDY	TIERNEY
KILLIAN	TULLY
LACEY	WARD
LAUGHLIN	WHALEN
LOGAN	WILEY/WYLIE
MAGEE	

PLACE NAMES

Another group of names in the forefront of fashion not only connote a place, as most strongly ethnic names do, but actually denote one. Place names have made enormous gains in popularity recently, and will probably make even greater strides since two star babies born last year—Melanie Griffith and Don Johnson's new daughter and Melissa Gilbert's new son—were both named Dakota. One more down-to-earth young mother told us the best place to look for interesting baby names is not in a book, but on a map.

Most of these place names are exclusively female, some are

ambisexual, and a few are still most often used for boys.
Among the most popular are:

G I R L S

ASIA
CAROLINA
CATALINA
CHINA
EDEN
EGYPT
ELBA
FLORIDA
FRANCE
GENEVA
GEORGIA

HOLLAND
INDIA
JAMAICA
KENYA
ODESSA
PARIS
PERSIA
SAVANNAH
SIENA
VENICE
VIENNA

A M B I S E X U A L

DAKOTA
DEVON
INDIANA
NEVADA

PORTLAND
SIERRA
TULSA

B O Y S

AUSTIN
DALLAS
DENVER

MACON
MADISON

Her first name was India—she was never able to get used to it. It seemed to her that her parents must have been thinking of someone else when they named her. Or were they hoping for another sort of daughter.

—Evan S. Connell, *Mrs. Bridge*

GIRLS' NAMES: SASSY . . .

Another cheery group we see as due for a revival is the wise-cracking waitress/smart-aleck showgirl contingent, not recently seen or heard from except on the late, late show in the movies with titles like *Maisie Was a Lady* and *Cain and Mabel,* made in the days when diners were diners and McDonald's was still a farm. Leading the way for this gum-snapping rejuvenation are little Mamie (Mary Willa) (daughter of Meryl Streep), Mabel (Tracey Ullman's daughter), and Fifi Trixiebelle and Peaches (children of Live Aid organizer Bob Geldof). While we draw the line at Toots and Queenie, we do foresee a bevy of little babes called:

BELLE	LOLA
DIXIE	LULU
DORA	MABEL
FIFI	MAE
FRITZI	MAGGIE
JOSIE	MAISIE
KITTY	MAMIE

MILLIE   RUBY
MITZI   STELLA
PATSY   TESS
PEG   TRIXIE
ROSIE   WINNIE
ROXY

. . . AND SWEET

Continuing in the fragrant wake of such So Far In They're Out favorites as Jessica, Melissa, and Amanda, but with an offbeat charm that could make them the good-girl cousins of Fifi and Josie, are the delicate floral names, last popular at the turn of the century. Rose and Lily have already bloomed. Also due for a revival are:

CAMELIA   MAGNOLIA
CLOVER   MARIGOLD
DAHLIA   ORCHID
DAISY   POPPY
FLORA   POSEY
HYACINTH   ROSE
IVY   TANSY
JASMINE   VIOLET
LAUREL   ZINNIA
LILY

The names in the next group go beyond sweet and innocent to virtuous. These are the Puritan "virtue names," out of

fashion for at least a century and a half but poised for rejuvenation along with Shaker simplicity and a feel for the classics and tradition. We're not suggesting anything as extreme
as the Pilgrim names made up of entire Biblical verses, such
as I-Walk-in-the-Valley-of-the-Shadow-of-Death Smith, but
perhaps the time has come for such unadorned statements
as, "I want a child who will be the living incarnation of this
attribute."

AMITY	GRACE
CHARITY	HONOR
COMFORT	HOPE
CONSTANCE	MODESTY
FAITH	PATIENCE
FELICITY	PRUDENCE
FORTUNE	VERITY

REJUVENATED TRADITIONS

It seems as if America is at last ready to rediscover names
rooted in the antebellum South—those used for blacks as well
as for whites. A hundred years late, we're finally abolishing
the taboo on slave names. In England, where there is no such
shameful history to "forget," names like Dinah and Jemima
are fashionably bestowed upon young ladies. These beautiful
names—some Biblical in origin, some classical—deserve to be
liberated and channeled back into the mainstream in this
country as well. Overdue for recognition are:

G I R L S

BETHIA	ELIZA
CLEMENTINE	JEMIMA
CLEO	KEZIA(H)
DELIA	LETHIA
DELILAH	ODELIA
DINAH	SUKEY
DULCY	

B O Y S

AMOS	LUCIUS
CATO	OCTAVIUS
ELIJAH	RUFUS

Ashley, Brett, Melanie, and even Tara have already been released, but there is another set of names ready to leave the plantation for America at large, some of which have been tied to its moss-covered image for too long:

G I R L S

AN(N)ABEL	SCARLETT
ARABELLA	SUSANNAH

B O Y S

ASH	CLEMENT
BEAU	DAVIS
CLAY	GRAY
CLAYTON	

BABY MEN AND WOMEN

It's time to get serious. This next group of names combines the brisk efficiency of the Androgynous Executives, the traditional values of the Restored Classics, and the unadorned simplicity of the Grandma and Grandpa names. These names aren't cute or cuddly, sensitive or vulnerable, frivolous or fashionable . . . quite yet. They are the names of the rich great-aunts and uncles who, ten years ago, you might have prayed would not ask you to name your child after them. These names definitely fall in with the armed camp: They're ready to withstand any adult battle that awaits them. So be prepared for an army of gray-flannel-diapered babies named:

G I R L S

ADELINE	FRANCES
AGATHA	GWENDOLYN
AGNES	HARRIET
ALMA	HAZEL
AUGUSTA	HELENA
BLANCHE	HENRIETTA
CLARA	IMOGEN(E)
CORA	JOSEPHINE
CORDELIA	KAY
CORNELIA	LETITIA
DOROTHEA	MARIE
ELLA	MATILDA
EUDORA	MAUD(E)
EUGENIA	MERLE
EVE	MINERVA
FAY	OLIVE

PEARL
ROSALIND
RUTH
SYBIL

SYLVIA
WILHELMINA
ZELDA

B O Y S

AMBROSE
AMORY
ARCHIBALD
AUGUSTINE
BARNEY
BORIS
CHESTER
CLIFFORD
CLYDE
CONRAD
CORNELIUS
CYRIL
EDMOND
FELIX
FLOYD
GODFREY

HAL
HECTOR
HIRAM
HOMER
HUMPHREY
ISAAC
ISIDORE
LLOYD
LOUIS/LEWIS
MOE
OSCAR
RALPH
SYLVESTER
WILLARD
WINSTON
WOODROW

COLD CASH NAMES

Most serious of all are the money names: Androgynous Executive names that not only hint at money but come right out and say it. You can't help but sound rich (we're only half joking) with a name like:

BARCLAY	MERCEDES
CASH	MORGAN
CHASE	PRICE
FORBES	PROSPER
FORTUNE	STERLING
GAINES	TIFFANY
GAYNOR	WORTH
GRANT	

ALSO NOTED

There are some names we couldn't quite squeeze into any of the above categories, but are nonetheless worthy of a fresh look. So here we submit for reconsideration a list we freely admit is subjective, eclectic, and eccentric:

G I R L S

ANASTASIA	ESME
ANTONIA	GENEVIEVE
ARAMINTA	JULIET
BERNADETTE	MIRANDA
CANDIDA	PRISCILLA
CASSANDRA	QUINTINA
DIANTHA	SYDNEY

B O Y S

ABEL	ASA
ABNER	AXEL
ANGUS	BYRON

CALEB	FERGUS
CALVIN	GIDEON
CASPER	JARVIS
DEXTER	JASPER
ELIAS	LEVI
EMMETT	MOSES
EPHRAIM	SILAS
ESAU	THADDEUS
EZEKIEL	TITUS
EZRA	TRISTAN

So far out they'll Probably always be Out

There are some names that are just too loaded with frumpy, dowdy, or nerdy baggage to come back into style now . . . or maybe ever. It usually takes three generations for a name to shed its moldy skin, and some of the names that follow have missed their chance. Others, popular just two generations back, may regenerate by the time our children have children. Right now, however, it's hard to imagine these names ever sounding fresh or cute or baby-appropriate again. On the other hand, if anyone had told us when we were growing up that Max and Jake would be among the trendy names of the nineties, we would have laughed them off the block.

G I R L S

BELVA	ENID
BERTHA	ESTELLE
EDNA	ESTHER
ELSA	ETHEL

EUNICE	MILDRED
FRIEDA	MURIEL
GERTRUDE	OLGA
GLADYS	RHONDA
GOLDA	SELMA
HESTER	SHIRLEY
HORTENSE	THELMA
IDA	VELMA
IRMA	VERNA
LAVERNE	WANDA
MADGE	YOLANDA

B O Y S

ADOLPH	HERMAN
ALVIN	HUBERT
ARNOLD	HYMAN
BERTRAM	IRVING
BURTON	IRWIN
CLARENCE	JULIUS
DEWEY	LESTER
DWAYNE	MARSHALL
DWIGHT	MARVIN
EARL	MAURICE
EDGAR	MELVIN
EGBERT	MERVYN
ELMER	MILTON
ELROY	MORTIMER
FRANKLIN	MORTON
GOMER	MURRAY
HARVEY	MYRON
HERBERT	ORVILLE

OSBERT

OSWALD

PERCY

RUDOLPH

SEYMOUR

SHELDON

SHERMAN

VERNON

WILBUR

WILFRED

WOLFGANG

FASHION LIMBO

There are many names that are decidedly not in, but neither are they out forever. These names—rarely chosen by contemporary parents—are in a suspended state of fashion limbo. A good many of these names were relegated to fashion limbo after being overused for and by our own parents. In fact, chances are you'll find your own name as well as your parents' names on this list.

Some of these names will undoubtedly be rediscovered by our children when they're choosing names for their babies. And we will undoubtedly be disconcerted by the idea of having grandchildren named Phyllis or Donald or Patti or Gary, just as our parents are dismayed at our own little Sams and Maxes and Rosies.

But other of these names will not fare so well (or so badly, depending on your viewpoint) and will pass into oblivion. RIP Rhoda, Myrna, Raymond, and Harold; here's hoping you don't rise again.

G I R L S

ADELE	GAIL
ANITA	GLORIA
ARLENE	HELENE
BARBARA	IRENE
BERNICE	IRIS
BETSY	JANET
BETTY	JANICE
BEVERLY	JEAN
BONNIE	JEANETTE
BRENDA	JOAN
CAROL	JOANNE
CHARLENE	JOY
CHERYL	JOYCE
COLLEEN	JUDITH
CONNIE	JUNE
DARLENE	KAREN
DEBORAH	LENORE
DENISE	LINDA
DIANE	LOIS
DOLORES	LORETTA
DONNA	LORRAINE
DOREEN	LUCILLE
DORIS	LYNN
DOROTHY	MARCIA/MARSHA
EILEEN	MARCY
ELAINE	MARGERY/MARJO-
ELLEN	RIE
EVELYN	MARILYN
FLORENCE	MARLENE
FRANCINE	MAUREEN

MAXINE
MINDY
MYRA
MYRNA
NADINE
NANCY
NANETTE
NOREEN
NORMA
PATRICIA
PAULA
PAULINE
PHYLLIS
REGINA
RENEE
RHODA

RITA
ROBERTA
ROSALIE
SANDRA
SHARI
SHARON
SHEILA
SHELL(E)Y
SHERRY
SONDRA
SUSAN
TRUDY
VERA
WILMA
YVONNE

B O Y S

ALAN
BARRY
BERNARD
BRUCE
CARL
CHUCK
CRAIG
DEAN
DENNIS
DONALD
EDWIN
EL(L)IOT(T)
ERNEST

EUGENE
GARY
GERALD
GERARD
GILBERT
GLENN
HAROLD
HOWARD
JEFFREY
JEROME
JOEL
KENNETH
LANCE

LARRY	ROGER
LEE	RONALD
LEON	ROY
LEONARD	STANLEY
MARTIN	TERRY
MITCHELL	TODD
NEAL/NEIL	VICTOR
NORMAN	VINCENT
RANDOLPH	WALTER
RAYMOND	WARREN
RICHARD	WAYNE

WHAT THE REST OF THE WORLD IS DOING

Style may in many ways be personal, but it's never isolated: A name's fashion status can be judged only in relation to society in general. That's why we take a look here at what the rest of the world is doing about names. You'll find lists of the most popular boys' and girls' names in the United States. You'll see what the rich, famous, and royal—often the trend-setters in all manner of style—are naming their children. And you'll get an insight into how famous names, both real and fictional, have inspired naming trends or else taken a name forever off the general market.

THE TWENTY-FIVE MOST POPULAR GIRLS' AND BOYS' NAMES IN THE UNITED STATES

It's tough to get a truly accurate tally of which names are most popular in the United States: The federal government doesn't keep any statistics; neither do national agencies like the Census Bureau, or many state governments. In fact, we were about to fling up our hands in frustration when we stumbled upon Fred Krantz, a research analyst for the state of Wisconsin with a special interest in naming trends, who generously pointed us to the states that do keep accurate records on how many babies receive which names each year. With statistics from six divergent places, we've compiled the following list of the twenty-five most popular names in the United States for 1988. (Early 1989 reports that have come in—there is a considerable tabulation time lag—show some new names about to enter the list in some states; look for Cassandra, Hannah, Jenna, Miranda, Rachel, Derek, and Dustin.)

G I R L S

1. JESSICA	14. HEATHER	
2. ASHLEY	15. MELISSA	
3. AMANDA	16. LAUREN	
4. SARA(H)	17. AMBER	
5. JENNIFER	18. DANIELLE	
6. BRITTANY	19. EMILY	
7. STEPHANIE	20. CHRISTINE/A	
8. SAMANTHA	21. KATHERINE	
9. NICOLE	22. COURTNEY	
10. KAYLA	23. CHELSEA	
11. ELIZABETH	24. VANESSA	
12. MEGAN	25. WHITNEY	(tie)
13. TIFFANY	LINDSAY	

B O Y S

1. MICHAEL
2. MATTHEW
3. CHRISTOPHER
4. JOSHUA
5. ANDREW
6. DANIEL
7. JUSTIN
8. DAVID
9. JAMES
10. ROBERT
11. JOSEPH
12. NICHOLAS
13. JOHN
14. RYAN
15. BRANDON
16. JONATHAN
17. ANTHONY
18. JACOB
19. WILLIAM
20. STEVEN
21. KYLE
22. ADAM
23. JOSE
24. ZACHARY
25. BENJAMIN
    CODY (tie)

Happy Birthday, Jennifer

I know it must be startling to realize how common your name must be for this greeting card to have been printed, but just think how much more disconcerting it would be if it also mentioned your remarkable sense of style, your love of Baroque music, your impatience with bureaucracy, and your conviction that your thighs should be thinner.

Enjoy your white wine and chocolate cake!

—Message on greeting card, Cards by Boynton

. . . having to explain to his daughter Maude why it is not a good idea to change her name to Tiffany: "Tiffanys don't last that long. That name is the leading killer of young women today."

—Walter Goodman's review of the TV show
FM, The New York Times

Well, the current list of favorite names for babies is out, and it's interesting to note that in the year 2057, nursing homes will be inhabited by the likes of Nicole, Megan, Lauren, Jason, Ryan, and Lindsay.

It will seem weird having a retired handyman named Ashley, a nun named Freedom and a doctor with the first name of Amiracle, but those are the current choices.

—Erma Bombeck, Los Angeles *Times* Syndicate

WHAT A DIFFERENCE A STATE MAKES

Why is Kyle the ninth most popular boy's name in Wisconsin and not even in the top twenty in New York, California, West Virginia, Idaho, or South Carolina? And what makes Vanessa a hit in California but a flop in New York?

While the standing of many popular names remains consistent from state to state, there are some wide variations.

In New York, for example, Joseph is the number-five boy's name, but isn't to be found in the top ten of any other state we surveyed. Conversely, New Yorkers place Joshua way down at number sixteen, while two Southern states, South Carolina and West Virginia, put it at the very top. Idahoans shun the Restored Classic Elizabeth, in the top twenty of all our other five states, while South Carolina is the only one in which Charles is in favor at the moment.

Sophisticated New Yorkers single out Alexandra, while South Carolinians favor Mary and Crystal, and Idaho parents like Lindsay. Kayla, one of the hottest new names across the country, has not yet hit either California or New York.

What does this mean for you? In general, if you want either a widely used or an unusual name, be ruled more by local than national popularity of names. Some cities and states keep their own tallies of most popular names and the results are usually published in the newspaper. Other methods for gauging a name's local popularity are asking your obstetrician or prospective pediatrician what other people in your area are naming their babies, making friends with neighbors who have kids in nursery school (and who often have a firm handle of naming trends), and loitering in your neighborhood playground. And if you live in New York and name your daughter Amber to be different, don't move to California.

Girls are more apt to be given unique or one-of-a-kind names than boys. There were 1,331 variations for boys' names and 2,061 variations for girls' names. In 1988, 871 or 8% of male names were used only once, compared to 1,361 or 13% for girls. On the boys' side there was a little bully named Angus, a Billy James and a Billy Ray but no Billy Bob, a Crit and a Britt, a DJ and an LJ, an Elvis and a Fabian, six Rockies but no Rambo; they ended up with a Zak, a Zeb and Zig . . . The girls had an Attaleigh and a Bradleigh, a Dove and 10 Robins . . . 47 Aprils, a May, no Junes, 33 Julies and a September. The girls also had a Piedad, a Seaira and a Siara, a Skye and a Sky, a Starsha and a Stasha, followed by Typhani, Xenia and Zgermal.

Some names showed up on both sides of the ledger. There was a little boy Angel and 19 girl Angels, whose parents will probably want to change their names when they hit the "terrible twos." There were three male Brooks and 33 female Brookes; one Dusty boy and seven Dusty girls; a Summer boy and 12 Summer girls. But the two Winters were girls.

—Chuck Bailey, State Registrar
West Virginia State Department of Health

It's a fact. Names come "in" and go "out"
again. The Johns and Marys, Barbaras and
Georges, Dorothys and Charleses have en-
joyed a good run. We liked them so much, we
used to give our dogs human names like Harry,
Kate, and Jack. I suppose now we can expect
to hear, "Come on in, Brandon, I'm getting
cold." "Heel, Jessica." "Stay, Melissa."
"Don't drink out of the toilet, Jonathan."

—Erma Bombeck, Los Angeles *Times* Syndicate

STAR BABIES

Their births are announced on the six o'clock news, their
pictures soon appear in magazines, and their names stand a
chance of being in the papers for the rest of their lives.

They are the children of celebrities, and the names their
famous parents choose for them are the essence of style. Mom
and dad live in a sophisticated, glamorous environment where
being fashionable—in everything down to your child's name—
is de rigueur. And if the stars aren't following fashion, they
are initiating it: Unusual names can become stylish after
they're chosen by even a single superstar for his or her child.
Cybill Shepherd's use of Clementine, for example, put an
instant gloss on that old miner's daughter's name.

Given that, it's not surprising that the following list reads
like an amalgam of the So Far Out They're In and the So

Far In They're Out groups. Recent additions to the far-out side include Bruce Willis and Demi Moore's Rumer Glenn, David Byrne's Malu Valentine, and Robin Williams's Zelda. Hot names among the Hollywood crowd include Annie, Hannah, Katherine/Kate, and Lily for girls; Jack, Jake, Max, and Sam for boys; and Alex or Jesse/Jessie for either sex.

For the most part, we've restricted our list to children born in the last decade to well-known celebrities. Middle names appear when they were accessible. Also, we realize that none of these children arrived without both a mother and a father, and offer our apologies to those lesser-known parents who might not have received billing here.

Star Babies Names

AISHA	Stevie Wonder
ALEX	William Hurt
ALEX	Lindsay Wagner
ALEXA RAY	Christie Brinkley and Billy Joel
ALEXANDER	Melanie Griffith
ALEXANDRA (SASHA)	Jessica Lange and Mikhail Barishnykov
ALEXANDRA	Christopher Reeve
ALEXANDRA BEATRIS	Tyne Daly and Georg Stanford Brown
ALEXANDRIA	Keith Richards and Patti Hanson
ALEXIS	Ted Danson
AMANDA	Ed Begley, Jr.
ANNA KATE	John Denver

ANNABEL	Lynn Redgrave
ANNIE	Kevin Costner
ANNIE	Jamie Lee Curtis and Christopher Guest
ANNIE MAUDE	Glenn Close
ARNE ROSS	Diana Ross
AUSTIN DEVEREUX (boy)	Michelle Phillips
BARBARA (triplet)	Richard Thomas
BARTHOLOMEW	Timothy Bottoms
BEN	Jeff Daniels
BENJAMIN	Raul Julia
BENJAMIN	Richard Dreyfuss
BIJOUX (girl)	John Phillips and Genevieve Waite
BLAKE AMANDA	Ron Perlman
BOSTON (boy)	Season Hubley and Kurt Russell
BRAWLEY KING	Nick Nolte
BRIGITTE MICHAEL	Sting
BYRON	Mel Harris
CADE RICHMOND (boy)	Keith Carradine
CAITLIN	Shaun Cassidy
CALEY (girl)	Chevy Chase
CAMERA (girl)	Arthur Ashe
CAMERON MORRELL (boy)	Michael Douglas
CARLY	John Ritter
CHARLIE	Mary Steenburgen and Malcolm McDowell
CHARLIE	Ed Asner

CHARLIE....................	Susan St. James and Dick Ebersole
CHARLOTTE ROSE ...	Rickie Lee Jones
CHESARE	Sonny Bono
CHLOE	Candice Bergen and Louis Malle
CHLOE ROSE	Olivia Newton-John
CHRISTIAN (twin)......	Mel Gibson
CHRISTOPHER	Kenny Rogers
CLEMENTINE.............	Cybill Shepherd
CLIFFORD	Ken Olin and Patricia Wettig
CODY (boy).................	Kenny Loggins
CODY NEWTON (boy)	Kathie Lee and Frank Gifford
COLIN	Tom Hanks
CONDOLA PHYLEA...	Phylicia and Ahmad Rashad
CONOR	Eric Clapton
CROSBY (boy).............	Kenny Loggins
CYDNEY CATHALENE..........	Chevy Chase
CYRUS ZACHARIAH (twin)	Cybill Shepherd
DAKOTA (boy)............	Melanie Griffith and Don Johnson
DAKOTA MAYI (girl) .	Melissa Gilbert
DASHIELL	Harry Anderson
DIAMOND NICOLE ...	Darryl Strawberry
DIMITRI	Ursula Andress and Harry Hamlin
DORIAN HENRY........	Lindsay Wagner

DREE LOUISE.............	Mariel Hemingway
DUSTIN (girl, twin).....	Debby Boone
DYLAN (girl)	Mia Farrow
EDWARD (twin)..........	Mel Gibson
ELETTRA....................	Isabella Rossellini
ELIZABETH	Tom Hanks
ELIZABETH SCARLETT..............	Mick Jagger and Jerry Hall
EMANUEL NOAH......	Debra Winger and Timothy Hutton
EMILY	Chevy Chase
EMILY	Richard Dreyfuss
ETHAN.......................	Jackson Browne
EVA FAY	Harry Anderson
EVA MARIA LIVIA....	Susan Sarandon
FIFI TRIXIEBELLE.......	Bob Geldof
FLEETWOOD STARR.	Tom Robbins
GABRIELLE (twin).......	Debby Boone
GASTON	Jaclyn Smith
GILLIAN CATHERINE	Patty Hearst
GRACE	Rhea Perlman and Danny DeVito
GRACE JANE	Meryl Streep
GWYNETH (triplet).....	Richard Thomas
HANNAH...................	Mel Gibson
HANNAH...................	Tom Selleck and Jilly Mack
HANNAH JANE.........	Jessica Lange and Sam Shepard
HARPER (boy).............	Paul Simon
HAYLEY ROSE	Jeff Bridges

HENRY	Meryl Streep
HOMER	Bill Murray
ISAAC	Mandy Patinkin
ISABELLE	Jeff Bridges
JACK...........................	Ellen Barkin and Gabriel Byrne
JACK...........................	Susan Sarandon and Tim Robbins
JACK...........................	Willem Dafoe and Elizabeth LeCompte
JACK...........................	Lesley-Anne Down and William Friedkin
JACKSON FREDERICK.............	Patti Smith
JACOB	Dustin Hoffman
JACOB	Rhea Perlman and Danny DeVito
JAKE	Sting
JAKE	Blythe Danner
JAMES CLIFFORD	Lynda Carter
JAMES LEROY AUGUSTIN.............	Mick Jagger and Jerry Hall
JASON	John Ritter
JAZMIN	Julius "Dr. J" Irving
JENNIFER	Billy Crystal
JESSE (boy).................	Don Johnson and Patti D'Arbanville
JESSE PARIS (girl).......	Patti Smith
JESSICA......................	Jeff Bridges
JESSICA GRACE	Joe Namath
JESSIE BELLE..............	John Denver
JOCELYN (twin)	Ron Howard

JOE..............................	Kevin Costner
JOE..............................	Sting
JOHNNIE.....................	Kris Kristofferson
JORDAN ALEXANDER	Debby Boone
JORDAN ELIZABETH.	Cheryl Ladd
JOSIE	Brooke Adams
JULIANA	Shelley Long
JUSTICE (girl)	John Cougar Mellencamp
KATE	Sting
KATE	Ted Danson
KATE	Meredith Baxter-Birney and David Birney
KATE GARRY	Goldie Hawn and Bill Hudson
KATHARINE JANE (KATIE)	Jane Seymour
KATHERINE	Martin Short
KATHERINE EUNICE.	Maria Shriver and Arnold Schwarzenegger
KATIE	George Lucas
KEITA	Stevie Wonder
KEVIN JOHN	Tatum O'Neal and John McEnroe
LANGLEY FOX (girl) ...	Mariel Hemingway
LIAM	Faye Dunaway and Terry O'Neill
LILLIE	Phil Collins

LILLIE	Mary Steenburgen and Malcolm McDowell
LILY	Jill Clayburgh and David Rabe
LILY	Kevin Costner
LINDSAY (girl)	Billy Crystal
LORCAN (boy)	Peter O'Toole
LORRAINE BROUSSARD	Jack Nicholson
LUCIE	Rhea Perlman and Danny DeVito
LUKE	Bill Murray
LYDIA MARIE	Patty Hearst
LYRIC (girl)	Robby Benson and Karla DeVito
MABLE ELLEN............	Tracey Ullman
MADELINE	Mel Harris
MALU VALENTINE ...	David Byrne
MARCUS.....................	Brigitte Neilsen and Mark Gastineau
MARY WILLA	Meryl Streep
MATILDA....................	Rachel Ward and Bryan Brown
MATTHEW.................	Christopher Reeve
MAX	Dustin Hoffman
MAX	Henry Winkler
MAX	Jill Eikenberry and Michael Tucker
MAX	Theresa Russell and Nicholas Roeg
MAX SAMUEL	Amy Irving and Steven Spielberg

MELANIE....................	Vanessa Williams
MOLLIE (twin).............	Meredith Baxter-Birney and David Birney
MOLLY	Mary Beth Hurt and Paul Schrader
MOLLY ARIEL (twin)..	Cybill Shepherd
MORGAN (boy)...........	Rae Dawn Chong
NATHAN	John Lithgow
NATHANIEL	Barbara Mandrell
NAVARONE ANTHONY..............	Priscilla Presley
NICK..........................	Ed Begley, Jr.
OLIVER......................	Corbin Bernsen and Amanda Pays
OLIVER......................	Goldie Hawn and Bill Hudson
OLIVER......................	Martin Short
PAIGE (twin)	Ron Howard
PALLAS (girl).............	Louise Erdrich and Michael Dorris
PALOMA	Emilio Estevez
PAULINA	Janet Jones and Wayne Gretzky
PEACHES	Bob Geldof
PERSIA (girl)	Louise Erdrich and Michael Dorris
PETER (twin)	Meredith Baxter-Birney and David Birney
PHOEBE....................	John Lithgow
PILAR (triplet).............	Richard Thomas
PRESLEY TANITA (girl)	Tanya Tucker

QUINTON	Burt Reynolds and Loni Anderson
RACHEL (twin)	Jane Pauley and Garry Trudeau
RACHEL ANN	Kathleen Turner
RAMONA	Jonathan Demme
RAPHAEL EUGENE ...	Robert DeNiro
RAUL SIGMUND	Raul Julia
REBECCA	Dustin Hoffman
REDMOND JAMES FAWCETT	Farrah Fawcett and Ryan O'Neal
ROBIN (boy)	Björn Borg
ROSE KENNEDY	Caroline Kennedy and Ed Schlossberg
ROSIE	Rachel Ward and Bryan Brown
ROSIE LEA	Roger Daltrey
ROSS	Diana Ross
ROSS (twin)	Jane Pauley and Garry Trudeau
ROXANNE	Ken Olin and Patricia Wettig
RUBY	Rod Stewart and Kelly Emberg
RUMER GLENN (girl) .	Bruce Willis and Demi Moore
SAGE MOON BLOOD (boy)	Sylvester Stallone
SAM	William Hurt
SAM	Michael J. Fox and Tracy Pollan
SAM	Sally Field

SAMUEL ROGERS IV.	Jessica Lange and Sam Shepard
SARAH......................	Kiefer Sutherland
SARAH EMILY	Joan Lunden
SATCHEL (boy)...........	Woody Allen and Mia Farrow
SCHUYLER ELIZABETH.............	Sissy Spacek
SEAN.........................	Pam Dawber and Mark Harmon
SEAN.........................	Oliver Stone
SEAN RODERICK.......	Rod Stewart and Alana Hamilton Stewart
SEAN TIMOTHY	Tatum O'Neal and John McEnroe
SEARGEOH (boy)........	Sylvester Stallone
SOPHIE FREDERICA ALOHILANI............	Bette Midler
SPENCER MARGARET	Jaclyn Smith
STATTEN JACK.........	Theresa Russell and Nicholas Roeg
SUNSHINE (girl)	Susan St. James
SYDNEY BROOKE (girl)	O. J. Simpson
TAMERLAINE	John Phillips and Genevieve Waite
TATIANA CELIA.......	Caroline Kennedy and Ed Schlossberg
TAYLOR LEVI (boy)....	Emilio Estevez
TEDDI JO (girl)...........	John Cougar Mellencamp

TESS	Jane Curtin
TESSA	Debby Boone
THEODORA DUPREE	Keith Richards and Patti Hanson
THOMAS....................	Jane Pauley and Garry Trudeau
THOMAS JEFFERSON	Britt Ekland and Slim Jim Phantom
TRAVIS SEDG............	Kevin Bacon and Kyra Sedgwick
TYLER........................	John Ritter
TYSON (girl)	Nenah Cherry
VIVIAN	Debbie Allen
WILLA	Lindsay Crouse and David Mamet
WILLEM WOLFE	Billy Idol
WILLIAM....................	Mel Gibson
WILLIAM....................	Susan St. James and Dick Ebersole
WILLOW AMBER.......	Roger Daltrey
WILSON	Christine Lahti
WYATT	Goldie Hawn and Kurt Russell
ZACHARY	Gregory Hines
ZACHARY	Robin Williams
ZELDA	Robin Williams
ZOE...........................	Lisa Bonet
ZOE EMILY	Henry Winkler

The Jack Pack

Baby Jacks have been sprouting up like bean-stalks. William Friedkin and Lesley-Anne Down's popped out of the box six years ago, when Willem Dafoe and Elizabeth LeCompte also hit the Jackpot. Susan Sarandon and Tim Robbins have a year-old Jack Sprat. Ellen Barkin and Gabriel Byrne had a little Jack-o-Lantern for Halloween.

—Angela Janklow, *Vanity Fair*

Yes, Woody is beginning a new era, with his little son, Satchel . . . Woody, I think it's a very nice name, I mean that sincerely; it's unusual, and I read that it was a tribute to Satchel Paige, a legendary sports figure. And Woody, I assume that some day Satchel will have a little sister, and her name will be Valise. Or Carry-on. Or Garment Bag. . . .

—Libby Gelman-Waxner, *Premiere* magazine

Much of the public believed when China [Slick, daughter of Grace] was born that her parents had named her "god." That was merely a Starship joke. As for her real name, China used to hate it. "But the more I've grown up, the more I've begun to like it. I think me and Moon and Dweezil [Zappa, children of Frank] and Chynna [Phillips, daughter of Michelle] are a lot more fortunate than people who got names like Mary or Sue or Ted."

—*Daily News Magazine*

Bette Midler on naming her daughter Sophie: "We wanted something that would go with the European sound of my husband's name [Martin von Haselberg]. We went around Cornelia and Chloe and Zoe and all through the Brontes. We think Sophie sounds like an impoverished Austrian princess who is forced to marry a coarse member of the French bourgeoisie. He doesn't have quite her delicate upbringing, but he has piles of money. That's the story we made up for her."

—*People* magazine

ANDREW AND ANNE, ATTORNEYS-AT-LAW

Among the children of the partners of one prestigious New York law firm, several names appear more than once. In order of the number of occurrences, the names in favor with the rich and conservative include:

G I R L S

KATHERINE (5)	ELIZA (2)
ELIZABETH (4)	JENNIFER (2)
MARGARET (3)	LESLIE (2)
ANNE (2)	

B O Y S

JAMES (7)	ALEXANDER (4)
CHRISTOPHER (6)	DAVID (4)
ANDREW (5)	RICHARD (4)
JOHN (5)	DANIEL (3)
WILLIAM (5)	PETER (3)

And two each of the following:

ANTHONY	LEE
BENJAMIN	MATTHEW
CHARLES	MICHAEL
GREGORY	ROBERT
JONATHAN	TIMOTHY

As proof that all is not sedate when law partners leave the office, we note the following names that break rank with the traditional pack. Included among the children of partners in the same firm are one each called:

G I R L S

ANYA	LARA
CHAYA	LUANA
EVANGELINE	MARIANA
LANDIS	MOIRA

B O Y S

AVROHOM	GARRICK
CARROLL	GRAY
CLAYTON	OGDEN
COLIN	PARKER
DONALDSON	SHERWOOD
DYLAN	

WHAT THE ROYAL ARE NAMING THEIR CHILDREN, or NOBLESSE OBLIGE

For the most part, the British royal family and peerage have limited themselves to a prescribed pool of sanctioned names. They seem to use as many as possible for each child, a fact Lady Diana must have been all too aware of as she stumbled over the litany of her future husband's names during their wedding ceremony. When the Prince and Princess of Wales had their own sons, Tyrone—or even Trevor—were decidedly not open options. The results: Princes William Arthur Philip Louis and Henry Charles Albert David. The Duke and Duchess of York, when choosing a name for their second daughter, were inspired by Queen Victoria's favorite granddaughter in selecting Eugenie Victoria Helena. Prince Charles's sister Anne went with the program when she named her first child Peter Mark Andrew, but proclaimed a measure of independence when she named her daughter Zara Anne Elizabeth. Some of the young royal cousins include Alexander Patrick Gregers Richard (Earl of Ulster), Lady Davina Elizabeth Alice Benedikte Windsor, Lady Rose Victoria Birgitte Louise Windsor, Lord Frederick Michael George David Louis Windsor, and Lady Gabriella (called Ella) Marisa Alexandra Ophelia Windsor.

Debrett's Peerage, the *Who's Who* of the British nobility, is brimming with the expected young Lady Victorias and Hon. Jameses; also popular among the present generation of junior aristocrats are:

G I R L S

ALEXANDRA	GEORGINA
ARABELLA	GILLIAN
BEATRIX	GWYNETH
CAMILLA	HARRIET
CAROLINE	HENRIETTA
CHARLOTTE	IONA
CLAIRE	ISABEL(LA)
CLEMENTINE	JANE
DAPHNE	JEMIMA
ELIZABETH	JESSAMINE
EMMA	JULIA
FIONA	KATHERINE
FLORA	LETITIA
FRANCES	LOUISE
FREDERICA	NATALIA

NICOLA	SARAH
OLIVIA	SERENA
PHILIPPA	SOPHIE
ROSE	SUSANNAH
ROSEMARY	

B O Y S

ALEXANDER	PATRICK
BENEDICT	PEREGRINE
CHRISTOPHER	PIERS
EDWARD	RICHARD
HUGH	RODERICK
IAN	THOMAS
JAMES	WILLIAM
JOHN	

This is not to say that British aristocracy is ready to surrender its reputation for eccentricity. Sprinkled among the Johns and Julias in *Debrett's* and *Burke's Peerage* are:

G I R L S

AGNETA	FILUMENA
ALBINIA	JENNET
ARIADNE	JESSAMY
ATALANTA	LAVENDER
BETTINE	LENKA
COSIMA	MABELL
CRESSIDA	MARIGOLD
DOUNE	MYEE
FENELLA	NINO

OOHAGH
PANDORA
PELLINE
PETREA
PRIMROSE

RHIANNON
SERAPHINA
SIBYLLA
TAMSIN
VASHTI

B O Y S

ALARIC
DENZIL
DICKON
DREWETT
EUAN

HAMISH
LOEL
MONTAGU
QUINTON
VICARY

Also of note are the names of the children of Monaco's Princess Caroline: Andrea, a boy, his brother Pierre, and Charlotte Marie Pomeline. According to unreliable media sources—but of interest here anyway—Caroline is in a "royal snit" because her father insists on calling her daughter "little Gracie."

THE SHIRLEY TEMPLE SYNDROME

In the early thirties, there was a sudden rise in popularity of the name Shirley, almost as meteoric as the fame of its dimpled inspiration, Shirley Temple, every mother's dream. Over the years, there have been other celebrities whose names (often not the ones they were born with) projected attractive enough images to appeal to lots of their fans when they became parents: Witness, for example, the legions of Debbies (after Reynolds), Judys (for Garland), and Garys (in honor of Cooper) born in our own generation. Unfortunately, these names can age and their popularity wane along with the celebrities who inspire them. The danger, then, of naming your child after a star is obvious: today's fashionable little Whitney or Brooke may be tomorrow's Shirley. Our list of celebrities who are influencing current naming trends would have to include:

AIDAN Quinn
ALEC Baldwin
ALI (b. Alice)
  MacGraw
ALLY Sheedy
ALYSSA Milano
ANJELICA Huston
BEAU (b. Lloyd
  Vernet) Bridges
BLAIR Brown
BROOKE Shields
CANDICE Bergen
CARLY Simon
CHRISTIE Brinkley
CRYSTAL (b. Brenda)
  Gayle
DACK Rambo
DELTA Burke
DUSTIN Hoffman
Bob DYLAN (b.
  Zimmerman)
HAYLEY Mills
HARRISON Ford
IAN Fleming
JACQUELINE
  Kennedy

JESSICA Lange
JODIE (b. Alicia) Foster
JUSTINE Bateman
KIRK Cameron
KIRSTIE Alley
LATOYA Jackson
LAUREN (b. Betty)
  Bacall and (b. Mary)
  Hutton
LINDSAY Wagner
LIZA Minnelli
MACKENZIE Phillips
MEREDITH Baxter-
  Birney
MIA (b. Maria) Farrow
MORGAN (b. Patsy)
  Fairchild
RYAN (b. Patrick
  Ryan) O'Neal
SAM Shepard
SAMANTHA (b.
  Victoria Louise)
  Eggar
SEAN (b. Thomas)
  Connery
SHAUN Cassidy

TIFFANY
VANESSA Redgrave

WHITNEY Houston
ZACHARY Scott

Other names, such as DARYL Hannah and GLENN Close, while not being used much themselves, are having the indirect influence of making male names more popular for girls.

STAR-SANCTIONED NAMES

When Brooke Shields confided to use about her Calvins, we all knew who (and what) she was talking about. While Calvin Klein may have made his name famous, it's not linked to his persona with iron chains, the way names like Thelonius and Tennessee (see "There's Only One Aretha," page 71) are bound to their sole owners. What we're saying is that the star-sanctioned names that follow are all viable options: There's no reason you can't have a little Calvin (or Flannery or Paloma) of your own.

ARLO Guthrie
AVA Gardner
BETTE Davis/Midler
BIANCA Jagger
BLYTHE Danner
BO (b. Mary Cathleen) Derek
BRONSON Pinchot
CALVIN Klein
CARSON Mac Cullers

CLORIS Leachman
CORETTA Scott-King
CRISPIN Glover
DASHIELL (b. Samuel Dashiell) Hammett
DINAH (b. Frances) Shore
EUDORA Welty
FARRAH (b. Mary Farrah) Fawcett

FLANNERY O'Connor
GILDA Radner
ISADORA Duncan
JACKSON Browne
JONI (b. Roberta Joan)
  Mitchell
KESHIA Knight-
  Pulliam
KYRA Sedgwick
LANA Turner
MARIEL Hemingway
  (named for Cuban
  bay where her
  parents used to fish)
MARLEE Matlin
MARLO (b. Margaret
  Julia) Thomas
MARLON Brando
MELBA (b. Beatrice)
  Moore
MERCEDES (b.
  Carlotta Mercedes)
  McCambridge

MERLE (b. Estelle)
  Oberon
MERYL (b. Mary
  Louise) Streep
NASTASSJA Kinski
PALOMA Picasso
PIPER (b. Rosetta)
  Laurie
QUINCY Jones
RAQUEL Welch
ROONE Arledge
RORY (b. Francis)
  Calhoun
SHANA Alexander
SHEENA Easton
SHELLEY (b. Shirley)
  Winters
TALIA Shire
TATUM O'Neal
TEMPESTT Bledsoe
TYNE Daly
URSULA Andress
WILLEM Dafoe

THERE'S ONLY ONE ARETHA

And only one Elton, Sigourney, Tuesday, and all the other
names listed here. What we're trying to tell you is that there
is not room in this world for two; these names are taken.
Giving one to your child is like sentencing her to a lifetime
of saying, for instance, "Yes, as in Sonny and . . ." These
one-person names include:

ADLAI Stevenson
ADOLF (the classic case) Hitler
ALFRE Woodard
ANAIS Nin
ARETHA Franklin
ARSENIO Hall
AYN Rand
BURL (b. Icle) Ives
BUTTERFLY (b. Thelma) McQueen
CHAKA Khan
CHARLTON Heston
CHASTITY Bono
CHER (b. Cherilyn) Bono Allman
CHEVY (b. Cornelius Charles) Chase
CLEAVON Little
CLEVELAND Amory
CONWAY (b. Harold) Twitty
CORBIN Bernsen
CORNEL Wilde
DABNEY Coleman
DEMI (b. Demetria) Moore
DENZEL Washington
DESI (Desiderio) Arnaz (Sr. and Jr.)
EARTHA Kitt
EERO Saarinen
ELDRIDGE (b. Leroy Eldridge) Cleaver
ELTON (b. Reginald) John
ELVIS Presley
ENGELBERT (b. Arnold) Humperdinck
EVITA (b. Maria Estella) Peron
GORE (b. Eugene) Vidal
GOWER Champion
HEDDA Hopper
HERMIONE Gingold
HUME Cronyn
HUMPHREY Bogart
JESSAMYN West
JUDAS Iscariot
JUDGE Reinhold
KEANU Reeves
KIEFER Sutherland
KEIR Dullea
LEVAR Burton
LEONTYNE (b. Mary) Price
LYNDON Johnson
MADONNA (Madonna Louise Ciccone)
MAHALIA Jackson
MARE Winningham
MCGEORGE Bundy

MCLEAN Stevenson

MERCE Cunningham

MERLIN Olsen

MONTGOMERY (b. Edward Montgomery) Clift

MOSS Hart

NENEH Cherry

OPRAH Winfrey

ORAL Roberts

ORNETTE Coleman

ORSON Welles/Bean (Okay, so there are two, but what do you remember about Orson Bean besides his name?)

PETULA Clark

POWERS Booth

REGIS Philbin

RING (b. Ringgold Wilmar) Lardner

ROCK (b. Roy) Hudson

RUDYARD Kipling

RUE McClanahan

SADA Thompson

SADE

SARGENT (b. Robert Sargent) Shriver

SEASON Hubley

SHADOE (b. Terry) Stevens

SHERWOOD Anderson

SIGOURNEY (b. Susan) Weaver

SOMERSET (b. William Somerset) Maugham

STOCKARD Channing

STROM (J. Strom) Thurmond

SWOOSIE Kurtz

TAI Babilonia

TALLULAH Bankhead

TENNESSEE (b. Thomas) Williams

THELONIUS Monk

THURGOOD Marshall

TREAT Williams

TRUMAN Capote

TUESDAY (b. Susan) Weld

TWYLA Tharp

UTA Hagen

VANNA White

VIDAL Sassoon

WAYLON Jennings

WHOOPI (b. Caryn) Goldberg

WINONA Ryder

WYNTON Marsalis

YUL (b. Taidje)
Brynner

ZERO (b. Samuel)
Mostel

When Annie Hall was pregnant, she once sat next to a man on an airplane who asked if she had thought of a name for her baby and, pointing to a page of the book he was reading, suggested Arsenio. A few months later, when she spotted the name on her own, she took that as an omen, and bestowed it on her only child.

—"Late Night Cool" by Michael Norman, *The New York Times Magazine*

There have also been fictional characters whom we all see as the quintessence of some quality—usually either stark black or white—to the point where what they are called becomes more totem than name. Ebenezer, for example, will always represent a bah, humbug! mentality, Cinderella will eternally wear a glass slipper, and Kermit will be forever green.

Other cases in point:

L'il ABNER
ALVIN and the
  Chipmunks
BARBIE doll
CASPER the friendly
  ghost

CINDERELLA
CLARABELL the
  clown
CONAN the Barbarian
EBENEZER Scrooge
ELMER Fudd

ELSIE the cow
FELIX the cat
FERDINAND the bull
GARFIELD the cat
GOMER Pyle
GROVER on Sesame
  Street
HAMLET
HARVEY the rabbit
IAGO
ICHABOD Crane
JEM is outrageous
KERMIT the frog
LINUS
LOLITA
Little LULU

MAYNARD G. Krebs
MYRTLE the turtle
OLIVE Oyl
OPHELIA
OSCAR the grouch
POLLYANNA
RHETT Butler
RUDOLPH the red-
  nosed reindeer
SHERLOCK Holmes
SHIRA, princess of
  power
TINKERBELL
URIAH Heep
WINNIE the Pooh

NEU SPELLINGS

The creative spellings of these celebrities' names have, for better or worse, become accepted alternatives. If you're tempted to follow suit and spell your child's name in an original way, check the dangers in "Catherine, Katharine, and Kathrynne," page 200.

ANN-MARGRET
BARBRA Streisand
BETTE Davis (the
  ambiguity of this
  name led to two
  camps of followers:
those who used the
French, one-syllable
pronunciation, and
those who used it as
a variant spelling of
Betty)

CAROLE (b. Jane) Lombard (the final E was a publicity man's mistake, but it led to a rash of babies named Carole)

CYBILL Shepherd

CYNDI Lauper

DIAHANN (b. Carol Diahann) Carroll

DIONNE Warwick

DYAN (b. Samille Diane) Cannon

EFREM Zimbalist

ELAYNE Boosler

EVONNE Goolagong

FREDRIC (b. Ernest Frederick) March

GEENA (b. Virginia) Davis

JACKEE Harry

JACLYN Smith

JAYNE (b. Vera Jane) Mansfield

JERMAINE Jackson

JIMI (b. Johnny Allen) Hendrix

JONI (b. Roberta Joan) Mitchell

KHRYSTYNE Haye

LEEZA Gibbons

MARGAUX Hemingway

PHYLICIA Rashad

STEFANIE (b. Stefania Zofia) Powers

ELECTRONIC INSPIRATION

There is little doubt that movies and television—TV in particular—have had considerable influence on naming patterns. Sometimes the effect has been immediate; often it becomes evident when the generation who watched certain popular shows as children and adolescents reaches child-bearing age.

The Westerns and hillbilly shows that rode the airwaves in the late fifties and through the sixties, for example, led to the hordes of city cowboys in the playgrounds of the seventies, to wit:

ADAM	Bonanza
BARNABY	Wagon Train
BART	Maverick
BEAU	Wells Fargo, Maverick
BEN	Bonanza
BRENT	Maverick
BRET	Maverick
CHEYENNE	Cheyenne
FLINT	Wagon Train
JARROD	Big Valley
JASON	Wanted: Dead or Alive, Here Come the Brides
JEB	Wells Fargo
JED	Rawhide, How the West Was Won
JEREMY	Here Come the Brides
JOSH	Wanted: Dead or Alive
JOSHUA	Here Come the Brides
LUCAS	Rifleman
LUKE	How the West Was Won
MATT	Gunsmoke
SETH	Wagon Train
SIMON	Rawhide
ZEB	How the West Was Won

With rare exceptions, such as Murphy Brown and Mallory on *Family Ties*, sitcoms and adventure shows are populated with mainstream-named characters—lots of Mikes and Maggies and Dans and Dianes. The genre that's taken over the reins from the old Westerns is the soap opera; many currently fashionable names—including Ashley, Amanda, Brittany,

Jordan, Lindsay, and Tiffany—were soap staples long before they approached popularity lists. The supreme example of the influence of soap opera on American nomenclature is the name Kayla. When the character of Kayla Brady was introduced on *Days of Our Lives* in 1982, you would have been hard-pressed to find Kayla in any of the current baby-naming guides. And yet, by 1986, with absolutely no other visible input, it had become the thirty-eighth most popular name in the typical Midwestern state of Wisconsin. Kayla has continued to climb ever since—in 1987 it was number ten in Tennessee and in 1988 an astonishing number five in at least two other states.

Other noncowboy characters who have made (and in some cases are still making) an impact would have to include:

ALEX	*Family Ties, Taxi*
ALEXIS	*Dynasty*
ALLISON	*Peyton Place, Search for Tomorrow*
AMANDA	*Scarecrow and Mrs. King, Dynasty, Days of Our Lives*
ANGELA	*Falcon Crest, Who's the Boss?*
ANGELICA	*Dallas*
ANJELICA	*Days of Our Lives*
ASHLEY (f)	*The Young and the Restless*
BARNABY	*Barnaby Jones*
BEAU	*As the World Turns*
BECCA	*Life Goes On*
BIANCA	*All My Children*

BLAIR (f)	*The Facts of Life*
BLAKE (m)	*Dynasty, The Guiding Light*
BLISS	*The Colbys*
BRANDON	*Santa Barbara*
BRANDY	*The Edge of Night, The Guiding Light*
BRITTANY	*Another World, thirtysomething*
BROOKE	*All My Children, Days of Our Lives, General Hospital, The Bold and the Beautiful*
CAIN	*Santa Barbara*
CARESS	*Dynasty*
CHASE	*Falcon Crest, General Hospital*
CLAIR	*The Cosby Show*
CLAY	*Search for Tomorrow, Edge of Night, Loving*
CODY	*Riptide*
CRICKET	*The Young and the Restless*
DARRIN	*Bewitched*
DELILAH	*One Life to Live*
DEX	*Dynasty*
DOMINIQUE	*Dynasty*
DORIAN	*One Life to Live*
EGYPT	*Loving*
EMILIO	*Days of Our Lives*
EMMA	*Kate & Allie, thirtysomething*

ERICA	*All My Children*
ETHAN	*thirtysomething*
FALLON (f)	*Dynasty*
FELICIA	*The Bold and the Beautiful*
FRASIER	*Cheers*
FRISCO	*General Hospital*
GWYNETH	*Loving*
HANNAH	*Anything but Love*
HARRY	*Night Court*
HOPE	*thirtysomething*
INDIA	*Somerset*
JAIME (f)	*The Bionic Woman*
JALEESA	*A Different World*
JENNA	*Dallas*
JORDAN	*Generations*
JOSHUA	*The Guiding Light*
JUSTIN	*Days of Our Lives, Search for Tomorrow, The Guiding Light*
KELLY (m)	*I Spy*
KELLY (f)	*Bachelor Father, Charlie's Angels*
KIMBERLY	*Diff'rent Strokes, Days of Our Lives*
KIRBY (f)	*Dynasty*
KRISTLE	*Dynasty*
LUKE	*General Hospital*
MACY (f)	*The Bold and the Beautiful*
MADELINE (Maddie)	*Moonlighting*

MOLLY	*Days and Nights of Molly Dodd*
NICHOLAS	*Eight is Enough*
NICOLE	*My Two Dads*
OLIVIA	*General Hospital, The Young and the Restless, Designing Women, The Cosby Show*
PAIGE	*Knots Landing*
PHOEBE	*All My Children*
REBECCA	*Cheers*
SABRINA	*Charlie's Angels*
SAMANTHA	*Bewitched, My Sister Sam, Who's the Boss?*
SENECA (m)	*Ryan's Hope*
SIERRA	*As the World Turns*
SKYE (f)	*All My Children*
SKYLAR	*The Young and the Restless*
SOPHIA	*Santa Barbara*
STEPHANIE	*Newhart*
TABITHA	*Bewitched*
TIFFANY	*Charlie's Angels, General Hospital*
TONIO	*As the World Turns*
VANESSA	*The Cosby Show, The Guiding Light*
WHITLEY	*A Different World*
WINNIE	*The Wonder Years*
ZANE	*Another World*
ZOE	*Somerset*

Soap Names

Often the same names—Jenny, Mark, Tony, Jason, Patty, Maggie, Amanda, and Kate—are given to characters on several soaps. . . . If something works on one soap (opera), there is no hesitation in adapting or blatantly copying it for another series. Names that are particularly descriptive of certain characters on a soap are used to continue that descriptive allusion on another one. Jennys, for example, appear to be women who are good and beautiful but often victimized between their triumphant moments.

—Seli Groves, *Soaps*

In March 1987, CBS introduced a new soap opera called "The Bold and the Beautiful." Among the leading male characters were a Ridge, a Thorn, and a Storm. Said John J. O'Connor in his *New York Times* review: "If nothing else, the names concocted for their characters are alone worth dipping into 'The Bold and the Beautiful' for a hoot or two."

MUCH ADO ABOUT NAMING

William Shakespeare drew upon Holinshead's *Chronicles* and Plutarch's *Lives* and Boccaccio's *Decameron* as sources of inspiration. Now it's our turn to draw upon his characters' names. Some of the most attractive:

F E M A L E

ADRIANA   *The Comedy of Errors*
ARIEL   *The Tempest*
BEATRICE   *Much Ado About Nothing*
BIANCA   *The Taming of the Shrew, Othello*
CASSANDRA   *Troilus and Cressida*
CELIA   *As You Like It*
CHARMIAN   *Antony and Cleopatra*
CORDELIA   *King Lear*
CRESSIDA   *Troilus and Cressida*
DESDEMONA   *Othello*
DIANA   *All's Well That Ends Well*
DORCAS   *The Winter's Tale*
EMILIA   *Othello, The Winter's Tale*
HELENA   *A Midsummer Night's Dream, All's Well That Ends Well*
IMOGEN   *Cymbeline*
ISABEL   *Henry V*
ISABELLA   *Measure for Measure*
JACQUENETTA   *Love's Labour's Lost*
JESSICA   *The Merchant of Venice*
JULIA   *Two Gentlemen of Verona*
JULIET   *Romeo and Juliet*
JUNO   *The Tempest*

LAVINIA *Titus Andronicus*
LUCIANA *The Comedy of Errors*
MARINA *Pericles*
MIRANDA *The Tempest*
NERISSA *The Merchant of Venice*
OCTAVIA *Antony and Cleopatra*
OLIVIA *Twelfth Night*
OPHELIA *Hamlet*
PAULINA *A Winter's Tale*
PHEBE *As You Like It*
PORTIA *The Merchant of Venice, Julius Caesar*
REGAN *King Lear*
ROSALIND *As You Like It*
ROSALINE *Love's Labour's Lost*
TAMORA *Titus Andronicus*
TITANIA *A Midsummer Night's Dream*
VIOLA *Twelfth Night*

M A L E

ADRIAN *The Tempest*
ALONSO *The Tempest*
ANGUS *Macbeth*
ANTONIO *The Tempest, Two Gentlemen of Verona,
    Merchant of Venice, Much Ado About Nothing*
BALTHASAR *Romeo and Juliet, Merchant of Venice, Much
    Ado About Nothing*
BALTHAZAR *A Comedy of Errors*
BENEDICK *Much Ado About Nothing*
CLAUDIO *Measure for Measure, Much Ado About Nothing*
CLEON *Pericles*
CORIN *As You Like It*

CORNELIUS *Hamlet*
DION *The Winter's Tale*
DUNCAN *Macbeth*
FABIAN *Twelfth Night*
FRANCISCO *Hamlet*
GREGORY *Romeo and Juliet*
HORATIO *Hamlet*
HUMPHREY *Henry VI, Part II*
LORENZO *The Merchant of Venice*
LUCIUS *Timon of Athens, Titus Andronicus, Julius Caesar*
MALCOLM *Macbeth*
OLIVER *As You Like It*
ORLANDO *As You Like It*
OWEN *Henry IV, Part I*
PHILO *Antony and Cleopatra*
SAMPSON *Romeo and Juliet*
SEBASTIAN *Twelfth Night, The Tempest*
TIMON *Measure for Measure*
TOBY *Twelfth Night*

IMAGE

As his name is, so is he.

—Samuel, XXV, 25

Every name sends out signals even before it's attached to a specific physical presence. It transmits subliminal messages and reverberations of its own: a level of energy, an intensity of color and sheen, a texture.

The image of the name you choose will precede your child throughout his or her lifetime. Strangers will use it as the basis for making certain assumptions about him or her: as someone intellectual or physical, attractive or plain, well-born or plebeian, unique or one of the crowd. Of course, your child's personality and presence will be the real determining factors in other people's judgments, but the power of a name to spar unconscious expectations is not to be underestimated.

The first names we will examine in this section are the ones we call the Power Names—those that conjure up someone smart or creative or energetic. The names in each of these three Power groups are distinct in tone and style, and your preference for one or the other will probably be clear, depending on your own hopes for your child's persona and talents.

Names can also project a physical image, not just of a person's attractiveness, but of the particular brand of appeal: sexy or pretty, refined or roguish. The force of names on people's perceptions of another's looks is well documented by studies outlined here, together with lists of names that have an attractive image.

Class is also an issue, albeit a touchy one, when it comes to a name's image. At any given time, some names are moving up the social ladder, improving their class standing, while others are moving down. Here you'll find today's upwardly mobile names, those that in the future can give your child a classy image.

Another image consideration is your child's position vis à vis his peers, how much his name will set him apart from the crowd or make him one of the gang. It's not difficult to pick the names at either extreme, but it's harder to define those that will help your child fit in and stand out. That's the list we present here. If you want to give your child an unusual name, will it help or harm him? We'll look at what psychologists have discovered about that. You'll also find a guide to names with images that may seem either too much or too little for a child to live up to.

And if the whole idea of a name's image defining your child appalls you, we offer here a selection of No Image names: those that have been used so frequently by such diverse groups of people that they present no clearly defined image of their own.

As the name Susie seemed too prim for a six-footer, she rechristened herself Sigourney, a name that she'd found in "The Great Gatsby." Her father tried to persuade her to drop this affectation, pointing out that it was a man's name and that she was mispronouncing it to boot: "It is SIGourney, not SiGOURney." But she refused to budge.

—*Premiere* magazine

If your baby is a redhead, or you're hoping it will be, you may want to consider these names that mean red:

REED/READ/REID   ROY
ROONEY   RUFUS
RORY   RUSKIN
ROSS   RUSSELL
ROWAN/ROHAN

POWER NAMES

The power of a name is often quite specific. Many strongly suggest a person who is particularly smart or energetic or creative. We have singled these out and call them the Power Names. Whether it is Intellectual Power, Creative Power, or High Energy, each has a potent image that can work for—or against—your child throughout his or her lifetime.

Some of this power comes from stereotypes: Martha the serious student and Bonnie the bouncy cheerleader. Sound also plays a part in imbuing names with power: Short, clipped names tend to suggest efficiency, for instance, while exotic or foreign names can have a creative, even a sexy ring.

Often, however, a name's power is drawn from more mysterious sources. But whatever its root, the image is unmistakeable. If you're in doubt, consider this: Of Helen, Kirstie, and Ariadne, who is the professor, who the gymnast, who the poet? While a Helen may very well do handsprings, a Kirstie lecture at Harvard, and an Ariadne negotiate loans, each will always be battling the image of her name.

Power names can be self-fulfilling prophecies. This is not because of some cabalistic force inherent in the name, but because it was chosen by parents who identify with the image the name projects. A painter and an actress, for instance, may prefer a name like Ariadne, with its creative undertones, over the kinetic Kirstie or the intellectual Helen for their child. Ariadne grows up in a house filled with her father's paintings, sees her mother perform on the stage, associates with the children of her parents' creative friends; is nurtured, in short, in a creative atmosphere. With that kind of background, she is likely to have a creative bent, no matter what her name.

Of course, naming your child Ariadne will not automatically make her creative. Power names say more about parents' expectations than they do about a child's talents. A child who has a different kind of power than her name suggests—the Ariadne who wants to grow up to be a businesswoman, or a gymnast—may feel, each time she says her name, that she is not what her parents hoped she would be. On the other hand, a power name can add dimension to one's personality with no effort on the part of its bearer. The numbers-crunching Ariadne, for instance, may enjoy being imagined "artistic" without ever having to set foot in a museum.

For their potential bonuses as well as burdens, you would do well to consider the following lists when choosing a name for your child.

INTELLECTUAL POWER NAMES

Names with Intellectual Power suggest someone who is not only intelligent but serious and studious.

The good news for these intellectual power names is that many are new arrivals on the fashion scene, which may actually be enough to make it cool to sound smart. Add twenty points to estimates of your child's IQ by naming her or him:

G I R L S

ABIGAIL
ADELE
ALICE
ANNA
BEATRICE
BERNICE
CAROLINE
CATHERINE/KATHERINE
CHARLOTTE
CLAIRE
CLAUDIA
CLORIS
CONSTANCE
CORA
DOROTHY
EDITH
ELEANOR
ESTHER
EVE
FAITH
FLORENCE
FRANCES
GILLIAN
GRACE
HANNAH

HARRIET
HELEN
HONOR
HOPE
IRENE
JANET
JUDITH
JULIA
KAY
LAURA
LEAH
LENORE
LOUISE
MADEL(E)INE
MARGARET
MARIAN
MARTHA
MATILDA
MIRIAM
NATALIE
NORA
NORMA
PAULA
PHILIPPA
PRUDENCE

RACHEL
REBECCA
ROSALIND
RUTH
SYDNEY

SYLVIA
THEODORA
VIRGINIA
VIVIAN
WINIFRED

B O Y S

ADLAI
ALBERT
ARTHUR
AUGUSTUS
BYRON
CHARLES
CLIVE
CONRAD
CYRIL
DREW
EL(L)IOT
FRANKLIN
GILBERT
GORDON
HAROLD
HENRY
HOWARD
HUGH
JUSTIN
LAWRENCE
LEONARD

LINCOLN
MARSHALL
MAXWELL
MORTON
NATHAN
NELSON
NORMAN
OWEN
PAUL
PHIL(L)IP
QUINCY
RUPERT
SAUL
SOLOMON
SPENCER
STUART/STEWART
THEODORE
TRUMAN
WALTER
WINSTON

Sorry, Dawn, But Doris Got the Job

Sexy is not powerful, at least when it comes to a name that will get your daughter a good job. So suggests a master's thesis written by Deborah Linville while at Rensselaer Polytechnic Institute, which compared the relationship between "sexy" names and corporate hiring. Linville's conclusion: "The present study indicates that there is a prejudice regarding women applicants based on the degree of sexiness of their first names."

Names considered too sexy for executives, according to Linville's study, are: Adrienne, Andrea, Cheryl, Christine, Dawn, Erica, Heather, Jennifer, and Kathy. Names destined for corporate success include Alma, Cornelia, Doris, Ethel, Mildred, and Zelda.

CREATIVE POWER NAMES

Creative Power names tend to display a certain amount of creativity on the part of their bestowers: They are often unusual, exotic, sometimes foreign-sounding, sometimes associated with an artistic figure. Pablo sounds more creative than Pedro simply because of Picasso. Names with Creative Power set your child apart from the herd; from the beginning, he or she is seen as someone special. Any one of those listed here would not look out of place on a theater marquee or a book jacket, in a dance program or a gallery guide. Encourage your child's creativity with a name like:

G I R L S

ABRA	CHINA
ADRIA(NA)	CHLOE
ALEXA	CLEA
ALLEGRA	CLEMENTINE
ANAIS	CLIO/CLEO
ANDRA	COLETTE
AN(N)ABEL(LA)	COLUMBINE
ANTHEA	DAISY
ARABELLA	DALLAS
ARDITH	DAPHNE
ARIADNE	DARIA
ARIEL	DARYL
ASTRA	DEIRDRE
AUDRA	DELIA
AURORA/AURELIA	DEVON
BARRA	DIANTHA
BETHANY	DINAH
BIANCA	DOMINIQUE
BLYTHE	DORIAN
BREE	DYLAN
BRONWYN/BRONWEN	ELECTRA
BRYN	ESMÉ
CAMILLE/CAMILLA	EVANGELINE
CANDIDA	FELICITY
CASSANDRA	FEODORA
CHELSEA	FLANNERY

FLAVIA
FLEUR
FRANCESCA
GABRIELLE/GABRIELLA
GELSEY
GEMMA
GENEVA
GEORGIA(NA)
GERMAINE
GISELLE
GREER
GWYN/GWYNETH
ILANA/ILIANA
INDIA
IONE
ISA
ISABEL(LA)
ISADORA
IVY
JADE
JAEL
JASMINE
JESSAMINE
JUSTINE
KAIA
KAYLA/KAILA
KEISHA
KEZIA(H)
KYLE
KYRA
LALLY
LARA

LEATRICE
LEILA
LELIA
LEONIE
LEYA
LIANA
LILIANA
LILITH
LILO
LILY
LOLA
LUCIANA
LULU
MACKENZIE
MAIA
MALA
MARA
MARGAUX
MARIEL
MARIS(S)A
MARLO
MARYA
MAUD(E)
MERCEDES
MICHAEL/MICHAELA
MINTA
MIRABEL
MIRANDA
MIRRA
NADIA
NATASHA/NASTASSIA
NEDDA

NATHANIEL	RAFAEL
NICO	RAOUL
NOAH	ROBIN
OMAR	SEBASTIAN
ORLANDO	SIMON
ORSON	SKY
PABLO	THADDEUS
PHILO	THEO
PHINEAS	TOBIAS
QUENTIN	TRISTAN

Creative class

Bennington College has long had the reputation of being a hotbed of creative activity. The following partial list of names of students, both male and female, enrolled there during a recent school year certainly reflects the creative activity of their parents during the naming process.

AMER	CHIARA
AMINA	CIARAN
ANDERS	DANIELIA
ANGHELIKA	DECLAN
ARIANE	DESIRÉE
ARIELE	EMORY
ARJUN	FAIZA
ARNIS	FAYNE
AURA	FELICITY
BARNABAS	FLANNERY
BERIL	GHAZI
BRENNA	GIBBS
BRYN	GIOIA

HYLA	MERILEE
IOANNIS	MIRI
ITALIA	MOLLIA
JOVITA	PARRISH
KAIJA	PIPER
KALEB	RAFE
KHEYA	RHODY
LARA	RIO
LARISSA	RUSHA
LELLA	SAVO
LIMORE	SCHUYLER
LORELIE	SEKKA
LYNMORE	SHONA
MACEY	SIMEON
MAIYA	TAMAR
MANAL	TAMARA
MARYA	VEENA
MAYA	ZARAAWAR
MERCEDES	

HIGH-ENERGY NAMES

Names with physical power—High-Energy Names—fairly cartwheel off the tongue, conjuring up a person in constant motion. A disproportionate number of these names end in a long *e* sound, consistent with adjectives like bouncy and perky. At their peak in the early sixties—during JFK's "vigor" administration—many High Energy names will still serve a child well. You should be aware, however, that there is energy and then there's energy: the competent grown-up kind suggested by names like Jill and Brady, and the pep-squad teenager variety personified by such names as Cindy and

Tammy and Jamie, which often prove not enough to live up to. The difference between the two groups is readily apparent, and if you want a supercharged image of either kind, consider the following:

G I R L S

AILEEN	JAN
ALI/ALLY/ALLIE	JILL
AMY	JO
ANNIE	JODY
BARBIE	JOLIE
BETSY	JOY
BONNIE	JULIE
CAREY/CARRIE	KEELY
CARLY	KELLY
CASEY	KELSEY
CHRISTIE	KERRY
CINDY	KIM
DEBBIE	KIRSTIE
DENA	LAURIE
DIXIE	LEXIE
DOLLY	LINDA
EILEEN	LISA
ERIN	LUCY
GAIL	MARCY
GAY	MELODY
GINNY	MERRY
GOLDIE	MIMI
HEIDI	MINDY
HOLLY	MITZI
JAMIE	PATSY

PATTY
PEGGY
PENNY
PEPPER
PIPER
PIPPA
POPPY
RANDI
RICKI
RORY
ROXY
SHARI

SHELL(E)Y
SHERRY
STACEY
TAFFY
TAI
TAMMY
TATUM
TERRY
TRIXIE
VICKI
WENDY

B O Y S

ARI
BAILEY
BARNABY
BO
BOONE
BRADY
BRODY
CAREY
CASEY
COREY
DERRY
DEVLIN
EGAN
FLINT
HARDY
HOGAN
IAN

JAKE
JAMIE
JEREMY
JESSE
JODY
KELLY
KERRY
KIP
KIRK
KIT
LEO
LUKE
MAC
MAX
MICKEY
MITCH
PATRICK

QUINN   RYAN
REGGIE   TERRY
RENO   TOBY
REO   TROY
REX   ZACK
RILEY   ZANE
RORY   ZEBEDY

BLIND DATE NAMES

Obviously it's beyond the power of a name to bestow good looks on your child—that, for better or worse, pretty much depends on genes, luck, and self-esteem. But a name with an attractive aura, like a good telephone voice, can influence other people's expectations and perceptions of someone's looks. Studies back this up: in one bogus beauty competition (see page 110), women of comparable attractiveness were rated with and without name tags. Nameless, the voting was even; when names became a factor, those with plain names were trounced by those with attractive ones.

An attractive name reinforces an attractive image, while an unattractive one contradicts it, can even throw it into question. We know a plain but charming man named Hunter who is wildly successful at getting dates, and admits he wouldn't be so lucky if his name were Melvin. On the other side of the coin is a perfectly nice-looking man named Herb who has, in desperation, resorted to introducing himself by his last name only—which happens to work as an appealing first name as well—and somehow doesn't get around to mentioning his given name until the third or fourth date.

ATTRACTIVE NAMES

Chances are, your sole criterion for a name isn't that it further your daughter's romantic career, but for better or worse, her name can have a lot to do with whether people see her as pretty or plain, foxy or frumpy.

Girls' names with a decidedly attractive image fall into two clear-cut groups: sexy and more delicately pretty. While a glamorous image, for example, will certainly spark your daughter's appeal on the blind-date circuit, you may want to think twice about the ways it will affect the other aspects of her life. Will Desirée make it to the boardroom? Studies say probably not.

The pretty names, however, carry less ambivalence. Some may be a tad soft, a bit flowery, but as a group they're more solidly grounded in the competent adult world.

Names that will arouse a certain anticipation in the opposite sex include:

S E X Y

AMBER	CLEO
APRIL	CRYSTAL
BAMBI	DAWN
BRANDY	DELILAH
BRITTANY	DESIRÉE
CHER	DOMINIQUE
CHRISTIE	FARRAH

GEORGIA
INDIA
JADE
JASMINE
LANA
LAUREN
LILA
LITA
LIZ
LIZA
LOLA
LOLITA
MARGAUX
MARLA

MONIQUE
RAQUEL
RITA
SABRINE
SALOMÉ
SCARLETT
SELENA
STORM
TAMARA
TARA
TAWNY
TEMPEST
VERONIQUE

P R E T T Y

AMANDA
ADRIENNE
ALEXANDRA
AL(L)ISON
ANDREA
ANGELICA
ARIEL
ASHLEY
BRETT
BROOKE
CHLOE
COURTNEY
DEVON
DIANA
EDEN

FRANCESCA
GABRIELLE
HALEY/HAYLEY
HEATHER
HIL(L)ARY
JACQUELINE
JENNIFER
JESSICA
KATE
KIMBERLY
LAUREL
LESLIE
LINDSAY/LINDSEY
MARIEL
MELANIE

MELISSA	PAMELA
MIRANDA	SABRINA
MORGAN	SAMANTHA
NATASHA	TIFFANY
OLIVIA	VANESSA
PA(I)GE	WHITNEY

Call Me Claudette

Whenever a new girl joined up, the first thing she needed was a working name. . . .

To me, certain names have always suggested specific images. A girl named Natalie should have long dark hair. Alexandra is tall and stately, and Ginger is a spunky redhead. I gave the name Melody to a girl named Carol whose voice was so mellifluous it made me think of music. When Wilma joined up, tall, sophisticated, and experienced, I knew immediately that she would be Claudette. . . .

These new names weren't only for the comfort and convenience of the girls, they were equally important to those of us who had to describe the escorts over the phone. When I or one of the assistants was describing a girl to a client, we would have to conjure up an image of her in just two or three phrases. Her name could be a big help in that process.

One day I had the bright idea of buying one of those *What to Name Your Baby* books as a way to generate more names. . . . I wrote down a hundred or so names that I especially liked and started asking the new girls to make their selections from that list. . . .

Occasionally I would have to veto one of their suggestions, because names like Monique, Noelle, Nicole, and Tiffany made a girl sound like a hooker. . . .

—Sydney Biddle Barrows with William Novak, *Mayflower Madam*, Arbor House

Pretty Name, Pretty Woman

If you were shown a picture of a beautiful woman and told her name was Bertha, would that actually affect your response to her looks? The answer is a resounding yes, according to research conducted by psychologist S. Gray Garwood at Tulane University.

Garwood staged a mock "beauty contest" on the Tulane campus, using six pictures of women who had previously been judged equally attractive. Three of the contestants were given "desirable" names—Kathy, Jennifer, and Christine—and three were given "undesirable" ones—Ethel, Harriet, and Gertrude. (The names' desirability had been determined by a student survey conducted by Garwood a year earlier.)

The results: Kathy, Jennifer, and Christine garnered 158 votes, compared to only 39 for the unfortunate Ethel, Harriet, and Gertrude. Not only did the men find the attractively named women more attractive; the women voters did, too! The contestants with the "pretty" names received 83 percent of the male and 77 percent of the female vote.

If parents really thought how much a name can influence a child's entire life, maybe they'd come up with better ones. Think about it. Is there a sex symbol named Erma? There is not! Is there a cheerleader in the Western world who answers to the name Erma? Get real. Are there any love songs, "Once in love with Erma"? Get outta here.

—Erma Bombeck, Los Angeles *Times* Syndicate

HANDSOME NAMES

Good-looking names for boys can be divided into two categories: nice guys and not-so-nice guys. The nice guys are sensitive and sweet and tend to offer a goodnight kiss at the door; the rogues don't call the next morning, although women usually wish they would.

To facilitate your son's romantic future, consider the following when choosing a name:

H A N D S O M E   N I C E   G U Y S

ADAM	JEREMY
ADRIAN	JORDAN
ALEX	JOSH
BARNABY	JULIAN
BEN	JUSTIN
BRYANT	KENYON
CALVIN	LOGAN
CAMERON	MALCOLM
CASEY	MAX
CASS	MILO
COLIN	NATHANIEL
ERIC	OLIVER
ETHAN	REED
EVAN	REX
FORREST	SAM
FRAZER	SCOTT
GABRIEL	SEAN
GIDEON	SIMON
GRANT	THEO
GREGORY	TOBIAS
GRIFFIN	TREVOR
IAN	TYLER
JARED	WADE
JED	

H A N D S O M E
R O G U E S

ADDISON	GRAY
ASH	HART
AUSTIN	HUNTER
BAILEY	JACKSON
BEAU	JASPER
BRADY	JEFFERSON
BROCK	JESSE
BRONSON	JUDD
CHAD	KEIL
CLAY	LEX
CLINT	LOGAN
CODY	LUKE
DALLAS	QUINN
DALTON	REX
DARCY	SEBASTIAN
DAVIS	SHANE
DENVER	WILEY
DEVON	WOLF
DYLAN	WYATT
FLINT	ZACK
GAVIN	ZANE

Overheard by Bob Smith on Macy's main floor, one female shopper to another:

First shopper: He sounds very nice. What's his name?

Second shopper: Bernie . . . [slightly

apologetic] . . . but he really doesn't look like a Bernie.

First shopper: So what does he look like?

Second shopper, happily: A Manny.

—Ron Alexander, "Metropolitan Diary,"
The New York Times

The name seems wrong for The Sexiest Man Alive—Harry is a name for an uncle, or a guy who asks you to the prom because his mother made him. Of course, Harold would be worse. So Harry it is. Harry Robinson Hamlin, to be precise—the Harry everyone's just wild about.

—*People* magazine

FITTING IN/ STANDING OUT

Picture a nursery school classroom. In the middle of the room is a crowd of ordinary children—those with readily acceptable, blending-in names: the Jennifers and Jasons, the Johns and Janes. Pleasant and convivial, but a little, well, boring. Around the perimeter, standing or playing alone, are the children with names that are unusual, invented, eccentric—the Ravens and Rains, Ivos and Ianthes. Interesting but risky.

Running between the two groups—now blending in with the crowd, now standing out as individuals—are the children with names that are recognizable, yet not epidemic; unusual, but not weird.

Choosing a name that strikes this balance, that will help your child both fit in and stand out, is difficult. Names that do so successfully seem to fall into one of the following groups:

- Less common forms of classic names—Eliza instead of Elizabeth, for instance, or Ned rather than Edward.

- Classic names not widely used today—Philip and Grace, for example.
- Twists on trendy names—Laurel as opposed to Lauren, Alec for Alex.
- Fashionable names at the bottom of the most-popular lists, like Chelsea or Jeremy.

Names we consider to have found this golden mean include:

G I R L S

ABIGAIL	GRACE
ADRIENNE	HIL(L)ARY
AMELIA	JENNA
BRIDGET	JESSA
CAMILLE	JOCELYN
CELIA	JULIANA
CHLOE	JULIET
CLAIRE	KELSEY
CLAUDIA	LACEY
COLETTE	LARISSA
DEIRDRE	LAUREL
DINAH	LEAH/LIA
DORIA	LEILA
ELENA	LILA
ELIZA	LILY
EMMA	LYDIA
EVE	MADEL(E)INE
GABRIELLA	MARA
GEORGIA	MARGO
GILLIAN	MARIETTA

MARIS(S)A
MAURA
MEREDITH
MIA
MIRANDA
NATALIE
NELL
NICOLA
NINA
NOELLE
NORA
OLIVIA
PA(I)GE
PAULINE
PHOEBE

POLLY
ROSE
SELENA
SERENA
SIMONE
SOPHIA
SUSANNAH
TAMAR(A)
TESS
TESSA
TOBY
VALENTINA
ZARA
ZOE

B O Y S

ALEC
AUSTIN
BARNABY
BRYANT
CALVIN
CAMERON
CLAY
CODY
DALLAS
DEREK
DREW
DUNCAN
EVAN
GABRIEL

GREGORY
GRIFFIN
HARRY
HENRY
HUNTER
IAN
JARED
JED
JEREMY
JONAH
JUDD
JULIAN
KYLE
LEO

LUCAS	SEBASTIAN
MALCOLM	SETH
MILO	SHANE
NATHANIEL	SIMON
NED	SPENCER
NOAH	TREVOR
OLIVER	TROY
OWEN	TYLER
PATRICK	WADE
PHIL(L)IP	ZANE
REED	

The best-liked names are those that are neither too common nor too unusual. So say a group of researchers at the University of Leicester in England, who have set forth the "Inverted U" (we would call it a bell curve) hypothesis. When names are either very familiar or very unfamiliar, according to the research, they are not very well liked, but at some intermediate level of familiarity, they achieve their peak popularity.

ODD NAME OUT?

To you, the name Waldo has worlds more character than William; Mabel is far more appealing than Michelle; Jessamine triumphs over Jessica hands down. But you worry about actually choosing one of these unusual, distinctive, even—

yes—eccentric names for your child. Will little Waldo grow up to be a weirdo? Will Mabel be a nursery-school outcast?

No matter how much a champion of the individual you are, indelibly singling out your child with an odd name is a scary thing to do. You don't have to rely completely on guesswork to address your fears: There is a mass of research on how unusual names affect children. Some of the results are comforting. The bad news, however, is really awful:

When a boy named Carroll goes bad, he goes really bad.

Not to say Carls or Christophers don't commit crimes, too; it's just that, all things being equal, Carrolls commit more.

So suggest Drs. Robert C. Nicolay, A. Arthur Harman, and Jesse Hurley, psychologists at Loyola University in Chicago, who, over a five-year period, compared court psychiatric clinic cases of eighty-eight white males with unique names (really unique names like Oder, Lethal, and Vere) with eighty-eight others who had common names. Both groups had similar backgrounds and had committed similar crimes, but those with unusual names had perpetrated four times as many.

"Unique names interfere with normal social interaction and . . . this produces disturbed adjustment," the psychologists conclude. "When a child is given a name that causes embarrassment or confusion as to sex (such as Carroll), is the object of ridicule (Olive), or connotes snobbery (Brentwood), he is going to have to fight for it and this may create emotional problems."

However, we must point out that parents who named their child Lethal probably did not train him for a future in the helping professions.

Berthas and Elmers may get lower grades than Lisas and Michaels, not because they're less intelligent, but because teachers are prejudiced against their names.

Psychologists Herbert Harari and John McDavid asked eighty elementary-school teachers in San Diego to evaluate essays of similar quality on a relatively neutral subject ("What I Did Last Sunday"). The researchers arbitrarily assigned and switched around first names of the fifth- and sixth-grade authors. Sure enough, papers said to be written by children with names like Michael and David received a full grade higher than those of Elmer and Hubert, while Karen and Lisa got a grade and a half higher than Bertha.

Eccentric names breed eccentric kids.

It's a chicken-and-egg question, according to more than one study: Nonconformist parents give their child an unusual name and raise him in an out of the ordinary way. The kid then tries to live up to his name—and his parents' expectations—by becoming distinctive or eccentric.

Before you cross every unusual name off your list of possibilities, consider the opposing evidence:

In real life, the academic performance of Berthas and Elmers, Lisas and Michaels, has more to do with their brains than their names.

Contradicting the "essay study" cited above, psychologists compared the first names of 24,000 students in a midwestern city with their scores on a battery of Science Research Associates (SRA) tests. The heartening conclusion: "[The data] clearly failed to support the hypothesis that unusual or unattractive names are generally or systematically associated with deficits in academic or social functioning.''

Mabels fare better than Waldos, but both may have as good a shot as any kid of doing just fine, thank you.

Girls are more apt than boys to find social acceptance and so avoid psychological problems because of having unusual names, according to research done at the Northern New Jersey Mental Hygiene Clinic by psychologists Albert Ellis and Robert M. Beechley.

Also, girls are more likely than boys to have unusual names, are more likely to find that other people like their names, and are more likely to score high marks on self-acceptance tests, according to Richard L. Zweigenhaft of Guilford College.

After carrying out a study in which he found that of those people listed in both the Social Register and *Who's Who in America*, 70 percent had unusual names and only 23 percent had common names, Zweigenhaft concluded: ''. . . in certain settings (such as the upper class provides) and with certain criteria (such as achievement), having an unusual first name does not have a detrimental effect and might even have a beneficial one.''

If you want to give your child of either sex an unusual name, we suggest you focus on another of Zweigenhaft's conclusions: ''Neither men nor women appear to be at a psychological disadvantage as a result of having an unusual or sexually ambiguous first name.''

The Real Reason Movie Stars Don't Live in France

French parents who give their children unusual names like Jade or Cerise are not just taking chances with their children's psyches; they're breaking the law.

An 1803 law drafted under Napoleon, who disliked eccentric names (wonder why?), gives the government final say over parents' choices of names. And if a name is "ridiculous" or "likely to provoke teasing," the court has the power to throw it out and substitute one it deems more suitable.

Judged illegal in recent years have been Prune, Jade, Cerise, Manhattan, and Fleur de Marie. Also rejected recently was, ironically enough, Napoleon—not because of the name itself, but because the child's last name was Lempereur (the emperor). Explained the mayor who turned it down: "We thought it would be just too hard for the little kid to take."

—*The Wall Street Journal*

Names are really important. In fact there's something I've never been able to figure out. When a child gets an unusual name, does he or she unconsciously try to live up to it? Or is a name a destiny over which he or she has no control?

Did little Fawn shred paper dolls instead of cutting them up with scissors? Did Tammy like to play dress-up and get into mama's makeup when she was 3? Did Imelda exchange credit cards as a little girl like some boys exchanged baseball cards?

It's my theory that the unusual name was deliberate because mothers thought it would take their offspring out of the ordinary and set them on a path bound for fame.

—Erma Bombeck,
Los Angeles *Times* Syndicate

CLASS STANDING

You want to give your child a name with class, a name that will imbue him or her with an aura of good breeding and refined taste. Even if you're not striving to create an impression of great wealth, at least you don't want to saddle your kid with a name that conjures up trailer parks and greasy spoons.

But class is a sticky issue, and a name's status on the social ladder is constantly shifting. Trying to cipher the current class standing of a name can be as difficult as figuring out how much money Donald Trump really has. A few general rules of thumb, however, will provide basic guidance.

- Most names of obscenely rich television characters (Alexis, Blake, Krystle) are downwardly mobile, as are names of obscenely rich real people (for example, Morgan and Whitney) unless you really are a Morgan or a Whitney.
- Also downwardly mobile are names of ridiculously expen-

sive stores or things: Tiffany, Bentley, or Crystal, for instance.

- On the other hand, names used for servants in 1930s movies about obscenely rich people are now upwardly mobile. Bridget, Josephine, Rose, Tillie, Amos, and Patrick have all arrived at the front door.
- Also climbing America's social ladder are eccentric names long favored by British nobility, names like Dinah, Jemima, Sophie, Harry, and Ralph.
- Names more obviously redolent of British nobility, like Amanda, Courtney, and Ashley, are downwardly mobile, however, as are names dripping with Frenchness—Michelle, Danielle, Nicole.
- Upwardly mobile are more homespun ethnic names—Irish, Italian, and Jewish favorites like Margaret, Maria, and Max.
- Also on the way up are plain, quiet names—Jane and John, Nora and Jack—that reflect the current status of conservative living and traditional taste.

These topsy-turvy rules are confusing, yes, but they are based on social principles that can be applied to other things— clothes, furniture, cities—as well as names. Here's how it works: The elite choose names sanctioned by their own social milieu, the middle class imitates the elite, and the working class imitates the middle class. But once a name filters down to the hoi polloi and becomes common, in both senses of the word, the classy image that sparked its popularity is tarnished and it falls out of favor first with the upper class, then with the middle, then with the lower. (Numerous examples of names that quite recently suggested an aura of class, of money and privilege, but are now downwardly mobile will be found in the section on names that are So Far In They're Out.)

The Upwardly Mobile names that are listed below are for the most part ones that have long been relegated to the lower rungs but whose image is rising, and rapidly. Previously in the mansion's kitchen or out in the fields, these Upwardly Mobile names are now more and more likely to be heard in the nursery.

Upwardly mobile names

G I R L S

AGNES	DELILAH
ALICE	DINAH
ANNA	ELLA
AN(N)ABEL(LE)	EMMA
BEATRICE	FLORA
BERNADETTE	FRANCES
BESS	GEORGIA
BRIDGET	HANNAH
CHARLOTTE	HARRIET
CHRISTABEL	HELEN
CLAIRE	HENRIETTA
CLEMENTINE	ISABEL(LA)
CLEO	IVY
CLOVER	JASMINE
DAISY	JEMIMA

JOSEPHINE
LILY
LOLA
MADEL(E)INE
MAE/MAY
MAGGIE
MAMIE
MARGARET
MARIA
NATALIE
NELLIE
NORA
OLIVE

PATRICIA
PHOEBE
POLLY
ROSE
SADIE
SALLY
SONIA
SOPHIE
STELLA
TESS
TILLIE
VIOLET

B O Y S

AMOS
BEN(JAMIN)
CALEB
CALVIN
FELIX
FRANCIS
GUS
HARRY
JACK
JASPER
LEO

MACK
MAX
NATHAN
PATRICK
RALPH
SAM(UEL)
SILAS
SIMON
TRAVIS
WILL

Names that are too Much, or not Enough, to live up to

Some names are so godlike, so heroic, that they could easily crush a tiny ego before it has a chance to sprout. On the other side of the coin are the names that even a toddler can transcend, names better suited to a parakeet than a person. Beware of giving your child a name that is either too much to live up to, or one he or she will always have to struggle to rise above.

Too much to live up to

ACHILLES	BLISS
AJAX	CAESAR
AMADEUS	CASSANDRA
ANTIGONE	CHASTITY
APHRODITE	CLEOPATRA
ARISTOTLE	CONAN
ATLAS	DANTE

DESIRÉE
FIDEL
GLORY
GOLIATH
HAMLET
HERCULES
JESUS
JEZEBEL
LAFAYETTE
LANCELOT
LAZARUS
LOTHARIO
LUCRETIA
MAXIMILIAN
MERLIN
MUHAMMED
NAPOLEON
OBEDIENCE
OCTAVIUS

ODYSSEUS
OPHELIA
ORESTES
PLATO
RADCLIFFE
RAMBO
REMBRANDT
RHETT
ROMEO
SALOME
STARR
STORM
TEMPERANCE
TEMPEST
VENUS
WASHINGTON
WELLINGTON
ZOLTAN

Not enough to live up to

BABE
BABETTE
BAMBI
BARBI(E)
BIFF
BIRDY
BITSY
BRANDI/BRANDY
BUBBLES

BUCK
BUD
BUNNY
CANDY
CHERRY
CHIP
CINDY
DEE
DODY

DOLLY
DOM
DUKE
DUSTY
FAWN
FLIP
GOLDIE
GYPSY
HY
IKE
JUNIOR
KIT
LES
LUCKY
MIDGE
MIMI
MINDY
MISSIE
MUFFIN
MUFFY

PEPPER
PIP
POPPY
RICKY
RIP
SHEP
SHERRY
SISSY
SKIP
SONNY
SUNNY
TAB
TAD
TAFFY
TAMMY
TAWNY
TIPPI
TISH
ZERO

I have one regret about my comments . . . about
the state of local news on New York television.
That is, my flip listing of some reporters' first
names. Reporters should be judged by what
they know and the job they do, not by their

names, especially since Tappy Phillips does a commendable job.

—Jeff Greenfield, letter to the editor,
New York

I always thought of myself as a star . . . I knew I was born to it . . . I think people are named names for certain reasons, and I feel that I was given a special name for a reason. In a way, maybe I wanted to live up to my name.

—Madonna, quoted by Stephen Holder,
The New York Times

No-Image Names

What do you think of when you hear the name James? It could be someone as sullenly sexy as James Dean or as smoothly sophisticated as James Bond. In other words, a James, like a John, Jack, or Joseph, can be anything. And, indeed, some names are chosen precisely because they project no specific personality. We asked two mothers we know why they had named their sons Michael, currently the most common boys' name in America. Both gave almost the same reply: With a name shared by so many different types of men comes a certain freedom for the child to be whatever he wants to be. Enough genetic destiny would be imposed on their sons, they felt, without the further constriction of a type-casting name.

But popularity is not enough to guarantee anonymity. Some of today's most-used names—in particular romantically feminine girls' names such as Jessica, Heather, and Amanda—evoke specific expectations.

Names that are truly "no image" tend to be those used

over long periods of time by parents from a cross section of religious, class, and ethnic backgrounds. Most are either short and unadorned or have so many nickname possibilities that there would be one to fit any kind of child.

G I R L S

ANN(E)	JOAN
BARBARA	KATE
CAROL	LEIGH/LEE
ELIZABETH	LYNN
ELLEN	NANCY
JANE	PATRICIA
JEAN	SALLY
JENNY	SUSAN

B O Y S

ALAN	MARK
ANDREW	MATTHEW
CHARLES	MICHAEL
CHRISTOPHER	NICHOLAS
DANIEL	PAUL
DAVID	PETER
EDWARD	RICHARD
JACK	ROBERT
JAMES	STEPHEN
JOHN	THOMAS
JOSEPH	WILLIAM

Mikes, Petes, Sams, Johns, Als, and Bills can grow up to be almost anything they want, while Keiths and Summers have to battle heavy odds to avoid careers in dental caps.

—Russell Baker, "A Name for All Seasons," Sunday Observer, *The New York Times*

[To my father] there were still numbers of names which hung so equally in the balance before him that were absolutely indifferent to him. Jack, Dick and Tom were of this class: These my father called neutral names;—affirming of them . . . that there had been as many knaves and fools at least, as wise and good men, since the world began, who had indifferently borne them. . . . Bob, which was my brother's name, was another of these neutral kinds of Christian names, which operated very little either way; . . . Andrew was something like a negative quality in Algebra with him—'twas worse, he said, than nothing—William stood pretty high— and Nick, he said, was the Devil.

—Laurence Sterne, *Tristram Shandy*

SEX

This section will solve all your sexual problems—at least in the area of naming your child.

Here is where we consider the gender implications of names—from the ultrafeminine to the tomboyish, from the macho to the wimpy—as well as the ever-increasing territory of ambisexual names in between.

When considering names for your baby, you may not have identified sex as the factor that makes one group of names sound appealing to you, another repellent. But most names do have a clear sexual identity, do suggest different degrees of masculinity or femininity. And the fact is that the name you select casts a distinct reflection of how strongly feminine or masculine you want your child to be and appear. If you are suggesting boys' names like Spencer and Miles, and your husband is countering with Rod and Clint, sooner or later he will accuse you of trying to turn your son into a wimp and you will tell him that's better than producing a baby who wears boxing gloves.

We are aware that the sexual reading of names can be subjective. Reactions will be generational (someone picturing the young Dorothy Lamour might wonder how that name ever got into the no-frills category) and individual (you dated a fullback named Dwight in high school and have forever after considered it the most masculine name in the world). You'll be surprised, however, by how many names—because of sound, style or specific connotation—have very distinct sexual profiles.

Your feelings about the sexual image of girls' names may be influenced by your stand on feminist issues. One father we interviewed said that in looking for a name for their daughter, he and his wife applied the following test: Does this sound like a prospective justice of the Supreme Court? As more and more women enter the work force, many parents are seeking an androgynous or no-frills name that will give their daughter an edge with the male competition.

As ambisexual names increase in popularity for girls, however, more parents are looking for traditionally masculine names for boys. While a name like Ashley sounds strong and capable for a girl, it has now lost a certain degree of power as a boy's name. Even the new manly names that reflected the sensitized ideal male image of the seventies are—and we think this may be a sad step backward—declining under the pressures of our brave new world.

One way to approach this section is to consider these issues first and find names that appeal to you and reflect your position. Another option is to draw up a list of names that you like and then use our classifications to make sure their gender implications are the ones you had in mind.

Either method will help you discover the kind of sexual identity you would like your child to project to the world:

the daintiness of a Cicely, the sultriness of a Selena, or the briskness of a Bess; the brute force of a Flint or the sensitivity of a Seth.

I find it entirely appropriate that Sofka should have named her sons after kings and emperors and her daughters as if they were characters in a musical comedy. Thus were their roles designated for them. The boys were to conquer, the girls to flirt. . . . Sofka sees her children's futures as being implicit in their names.*

—Anita Brookner, *Family and Friends*

*Those names were Frederick, Alfred, Mireille (Mimi), and Babette (Betty).

FROM MADONNA
TO MERYL

The sexual impact of girls' names seems to break down into four main categories:

Feminissima: The ultrafeminine, often sexy, sometimes fluffy female names, à la Madonna.

Feminine: Female names that suggest a classic sort of femininity.

No-frills: Straightforward names that, while clearly female, have an efficient, no-nonsense air.

Boyish: Names like Meryl that are used for girls but have a boyish or ambisexual image.

Here you'll find specifics on each of these categories, along with lists of names in the four groups. In addition, if there is a girl's name you like, but you're not comfortable with its sexual image, we offer a guide to modifying the name to make it fit into a more acceptable category.

Now I wonder what would please her,
Charlotte, Julia or Louisa?
Ann and Mary, they're too common;
Joan's too formal for a woman:
Jane's a prettier name beside;
But we had a Jane that died.
They would say, if 'twas Rebecca,
That she was a little Quaker,
Edith's pretty, but that looks
Better in old English books.
Ellen's left off long ago:
Blanche is out of fashion now.
None that I have named as yet
Are so good as Margaret.
Emily is neat and fine.
What do you think of Caroline?

—Charles Lamb

FEMINISSIMA NAMES

If these names were dresses, they would be pale pink, with ruffles and lace and big bows and sprigs of flowers strewn on every available square inch. They are the sweetest of the sweet, the most feminine of the feminine names.

What makes these names Feminissima rather than merely Feminine? Three or more syllables sometimes do it. Soft sounds—s's and f's—can also push a name over the edge from Feminine to Feminissima. Names that by their meaning suggest ultrafeminine qualities, like Allegra and Lacey, are Feminissima. Very exotic names—especially Latin ones like Raffaela and Gabriella—qualify. And sex-goddess names—from Salomé to Marilyn to Madonna—also connote an exaggerated femininity.

You can hardly give your daughter one of these names without suggesting a little girl with ringlets and rosy cheeks, the kind of child who plays only with dolls (with ringlets and rosy cheeks) and cries if her Mary Janes get scuffed. Her name will make boys want to go on blind dates with her, and other girls see her as a potential threat even before they meet her.

Does that mean that giving your girl a Feminissima name will automatically make her a spineless jellyfish? Quite the opposite. There is something modern about these hyperfeminine names, something liberating about the possibility of an Angelica being chosen vice-president over an Alix. Just as the notion of a female Tyler with long hair and high heels has the appeal of the unexpected, so has that of a Felicia in a business suit or sweat pants.

Feminissima names

ADORA	ANGELICA
ADRIANA	ANGELINA
ALEXANDRA	ANNABELLA
ALLEGRA	ARABELLA
ALYSSA and variations	ARIANA

ARIEL	ISABELLA
AURORA	JOSETTE
BABETTE	JULIANA
BARBIE	LACEY
BELINDA	LANA
BLOSSOM	LARISSA
CAMILLA	LETITIA
CAROLINA	LILIANA
CASSANDRA	LISABETH
CECILIA	LOUELLA
CECILY	LUCIANA
CHERIE	LUCINDA
CHRISSIE	MADONNA
CHRISTABEL	MARCELLA
CICELY	MARIETTA
CLARISSA	MARILYN
CRYSTAL	MARTITIA
DAWN	MELISSA
DESIRÉE	MELODY
DOLLY	MERRY
ELISSA	MIRABELLE
EMMALINE	MISSIE
EVANGELINE	MONIQUE
FAWN	ORIANA
FELICIA	PRISCILLA
FIFI	RAFFAELA
FRANCESCA	ROSALINDA
GABRIELLA	SABINA
GEORGIANA	SABRINA
GISELLE	SALOMÉ
HEATHER	SAMANTHA
HYACINTH	SCARLETT

SELENA   TIFFANY
SERENA   TRICIA
SUZETTE   VALENTINA
TABITHA   VANESSA
TAFFY   VENUS
TATIANA   YVETTE
TEMPEST

FEMININE NAMES

By far the largest group of girls' names is made up of Feminine names: names that are clearly female without being too fussy, sweet without being syrupy, soft without being limp. Many of the most popular girls' names of recent years can be found on this list. Style has favored these decidedly feminine names, along with androgynous names, over either ultrafeminine or no-nonsense female names.

The advantages of a Feminine name are several. Most of these names are easy to understand and easy to like: Your child will hear again and again what a pretty name she has, and that's pleasing. Also, kids like names that are sexually unambiguous; they like labels that clearly identify them as a girl or a boy. And most of these names are familiar, either because of their classic status or because they have been popular in recent times.

What of the future for Feminine names? Some, like Katherine and Elizabeth, are virtually timeless, but many of the names in this group have been so fashionable for several years that they verge on the cliché. If you want to stay away from a name that is already too trendy, be sure to cross-reference any you like here with the So Far In They're Out list in the Style section. One general observation: Many of the hypereuphonic feminine names—Jennifer, Christina, et al—are on their way out, while more offbeat feminine names, like Annabel, Daisy, Savannah, sound newer and stronger.

Feminine names

ABIGAIL
ADELA
ADELAIDE
ADELINE
ADRIENNE
AILEEN
ALANA/ALANNA
ALEXA
ALEXANDRA
ALEXIS
ALICIA
AL(L)ISON
AMANDA
AMBER
AMELIA
AMY
ANDREA
ANGELA
AN(N)ABEL(LE)
ANNETTE
ANTONIA
APRIL
ARAMINTA
ARLETTA
AUDRA

AUDREY
BEATRICE
BEATRIX
BECCA
BELLE
BENITA
BERNADETTE
BIANCA
BONNIE
BRIDGET
BRONWYN/
    BRONWEN
CAITLIN
CAMILLE
CANDACE
CARA
CAROLINE
CATHERINE/
    KATHERINE
CECILE
CELESTE
CELIA
CHARMAINE
CHELSEA
CHLOE

CHRISTA
CHRISTIANA
CHRISTINA
CHRISTINE
CLARICE
CLAUDETTE
CLEMENTINE
COLETTE
COLLEEN
CORDELIA
CORNELIA
CYNTHIA
DAISY
DANIELLA
DAPHNE
DARLA
DARLENE
DEANNA
DEBORAH
DEIRDRE
DELIA
DELILAH
DENISE
DIANA
DINAH
DOMINIQUE
DONNA
DOREEN
DORIA
DOROTHEA
EILEEN
ELAINE

ELENA
ELISE
ELIZA
ELIZABETH
ELOISE
EMILY
ESMÉ
EVA
EVELYN
FEODORA
FERN
FIONA
FLORA
FRANCINE
GABRIELLE
GAY
GELSEY
GEORGIA
GILLIAN
GINA
GLORIA
GLYNIS
GRETCHEN
GWENDOLYN
HALEY/HAYLEY
HELENA
HELENE
HENRIETTA
HIL(L)ARY
HOLLY
IMOGEN(E)
INGRID

IRIS
ISABEL
JACQUELINE
JANICE
JANINE
JASMINE
JEANETTE
JENNA
JENNIFER
JESSA
JESSICA
JOANNA
JOCELYN
JULIA
JULIET
JUSTINE
KATHLEEN
KEZIA(H)
KIMBERLY
KIRSTEN
KRISTIN
LANA
LARA
LAURA
LAUREL
LAUREN
LEATRICE
LEILA
LEONORA
LIA
LIANA
LILA

LILIAN
LILY
LINDA
LISA
LIZA
LOLA
LORETTA
LORNA
LORRAINE
LOUISA
LUCIA
LUCY
MADEL(E)INE
MARA
MARCIA/MARSHA
MARGO
MARGUERITE
MARIA
MARIEL
MARINA
MARLENE
MARYA
MAURA
MAUREEN
MEGAN
MELANIE
MELANTHA
MERCEDES
MIA
MICHELLE
MIRANDA
MOLLY

MONICA	PIA
NANCY	PILAR
NANETTE	POLLY
NAOMI	QUINTINA/
NATALIE	QUINTANA
NESSA	RAMONA
NICOLA	REBECCA
NICOLE	REGINA
NINA	RENATA
NOELLE	RENÉE
NOREEN	RHEA
ODELIA	RITA
ODESSA	ROCHELLE
ODETTE	ROSA
ODILE	ROSALIE
OLIVIA	ROSALIND
OPHELIA	ROSAMOND
PALMA	ROSANNA
PALOMA	ROSEMARY
PAMELA	ROWENA
PANDORA	ROXANNE
PANSY	RUBY
PATRICE	SABINE
PATRICIA	SABRA
PAULETTE	SANDRA
PAULINA	SAVANNAH
PAULINE	SELENA
PEGEEN	SERENA
PENELOPE	SHANA
PETRA	SHANNON
PHILIPPA	SHARON
PHOEBE	SHEENA

SHEILA
SHERRY
SHIRA
SHOSHANA
SIMONE
SONDRA
SONIA
SOPHIA
STELLA
STEPHANIE
SUSANNAH
SUZANNE
SYLVIA
TALIA
TAMAR
TAMARA
TANYA
TARA
TESSA
THEODORA
T(H)ERESA
THOMASINA

TILLIE
TINA
TRISH
VALERIE
VENICE/VENETIA
VERONICA
VICTORIA
VIOLET
VIRGINIA
VIVIAN
WENDY
YASMINE
YOLANDA
YVONNE
ZANDRA
ZARA
ZELIA
ZENA
ZIA
ZOE
ZORAH

NO-FRILLS NAMES

These are the denim skirts of girls' names: clearly not fit for boys, but as straightforward, down to earth, and—sometimes—blunt as you can get while still being female.

One readily apparent difference between these and the more feminine girls' names is that they are shorter: fewer letters and syllables, fewer embellishments. Many end in consonants rather than vowels, which gives them a harder sound. They're almost like generic labeling: Yes, they say, this is a girl, but that's all we're going to tell you.

The No-Frills names here fall into two groups: those with a straightforward sound—direct and to-the-point names like Jean, Lynn, Ruth—and those with a no-nonsense image: Constance, Gladys, Mildred.

While names from both groups have been out of favor for several years now, many are on their way back into style. Trend-setters are already adopting some of them: Sam Shepard and Jessica Lange's baby daughter is named Hannah Jane; Meryl Streep's daughters are named Grace Jane and Mary Willa, and Willa is also the name of Lindsay Crouse and David Mamet's daughter. We've heard of some stylish young Eleanors and Helens and Josephines as well.

Some of these names, however, are still struggling against a residual image of dowdiness, and you'll see them on our So Far Out They'll Probably Always Be Out list, starting on page 37. Others—Ellen, Carol, Barbara, for instance—are now in Fashion Limbo, and won't be due for a comeback until ranch houses and avocado green refrigerators are back in style. But with fifties blond-wood furniture selling for high prices in Greenwich Village, that may be sooner than you'd guess.

No-frills names

ADA
ADELE
AGATHA
AGNES
ALICE
ANNA
ANN(E)
BARBARA
BERNICE
BERTHA

BESS
BETH
BLANCHE
CARLA
CAROL
CASS
CEIL
CHARLOTTE
CLAIRE
CLAUDIA
CONSTANCE
CORA
CORINNE
DELLA
DIANE
DORA
DORCAS
DORIS
DOROTHY
EDITH
EDNA
ELEANOR
ELLA
ELLEN
EMMA
ENID
ESTELLE
ESTHER
ETHEL
ETTA
EUNICE
EVE

FAITH
FAY
FRANCES
FRIEDA
GAIL
GERALDINE
GLADYS
GRACE
GRETA
GWEN
HANNAH
HARRIET
HAZEL
HEIDI
HELEN
HESTER
HILDA
HONOR
HOPE
HORTENSE
IDA
INA
INEZ
IRENE
JANE
JANET
JEAN
JILL
JOAN
JOANNE
JOSEPHINE
JOY

JOYCE
JUDITH
JULIE
JUNE
KAREN
KATE
KAY
KIM
LEAH
LEIGH
LENORE
LESLIE
LOIS
LOUISE
LUCILLE
LYNN
MADGE
MAE/MAY
MAEVE
MARGARET
MARIAN
MARIE
MARTHA
MARY
MAUD(E)
MAVIS
MAXINE
MEG
MILDRED
MIRIAM
MONA
NELL

NOLA
NORA
NORMA
OLIVE
PATIENCE
PAULA
PAULINE
PEARL
PHYLLIS
PRUDENCE
RACHEL
RHODA
ROBERTA
ROSE
RUTH
SADIE
SALLY
SARA(H)
SELMA
SOPHIE
SUSAN
SYBIL
THELMA
TRUDY
VELMA
VERA
VERNA
WANDA
WILLA
WINIFRED
ZELDA

BOYISH NAMES

Whitney Houston has one. So do Glenn Close, Meryl Streep, Sean Young, Jodie Foster, Brooke Shields, Daryl Hannah, Mel Harris, Mackenzie Phillips, Michael Learned, Lindsay Wagner, Bo Derek, Drew Barrymore, Quinn Cummings, Barrie Chase, Norris Church, and Christopher Norris. Jamie Lee Curtis has two.

They're Boyish names, and they're increasingly popular for girls. Time was, women hid behind men's names in order to be taken seriously. But where George—as in Eliot or Sand—was once an alias, now it's more likely to be a girl's real name.

There is a long history of appealing heroines with boyish names: from Jo in *Little Women* to Lady Brett in *The Sun Also Rises*. In fact, there are dozens of leading ladies who have played a character with a masculine-sounding name at some point in their careers. Irene Dunne was Ray, for example, and Audrey Hepburn, Reggie; Tuesday Weld, Christian; Bette Davis, Stanley; Olivia DeHavilland, Roy; Janet Leigh, Wally; and Jane Russell, Nancy Sinatra, and Anne Baxter all Mikes.

Television loves Boyish names for girls: you can watch Rudy on "The Cosby Show" or Mallory on "Family Ties" or Blair on "The Facts of Life" or Alexis on "Dynasty." The night and daytime soaps are rife with female Kirbys, Sydneys and Blaines (see p. 78). And several celebrities have chosen Boyish names for their daughters: Sissy Spacek's little girl is named Schuyler, for instance, and Mariel Hemingway's daughter is called Langley Fox.

Sometimes, a name that sounds tired for a boy, like Sydney, becomes fresh and crisp when applied to a girl. Names that can be wimpy for a boy, such as Brooke or Blair, can confer a brisk kind of strength on a girl.

But Boyish names often appeal more to parents than to the child herself. A girl named Casey may be disturbed by the fact that her male playmate down the block has the same name, and wish she were called something more clearly defined as female, like Jennifer. However, most grown-up women with Boyish names say they began to be grateful to their parents for them when they reached the age of about eighteen. At that point, they started to appreciate the sexual ambiguity as well as the sex appeal of having a boyish name.

What follows is a list of Boyish names that are commonly used for girls. If you want to venture further into masculine-sounding names for your daughter, also consult the list of ambisexual names, starting on page 176.

Boyish names

ALI	BRYN
ALIX/ALEX	CAREY
ALLY/ALLIE	CARLIN
ASHLEY	CARLY
BARRIE	CARMEN
BERRY	CASEY
BERYL	CHRIS
BILLIE	CODY
BLAIR	COREY
BO	COURTNEY
BRETT	DALE
BROOKE	DANA

DEVON
DORIAN
EDEN
FLANNERY
GENE
GERMAINE
GERRY
GREER
GWYN
JAMIE
JAN
JESSIE
JO
JODY
JORDAN
KEIL
KELLY
KELSEY
KERRY
KIM
KIT
KYLE
LEE
LESLIE
LINDSAY
MACKENZIE

MALLORY
MEREDITH
MERLE
MERYL
MORGAN
NOEL
PAT
RAE
RANDI/RANDY
RICKI/RICKY
ROBIN
RORY
SACHA/SASHA
SHAWN
SHELBY
SHELL(E)Y
SYDNEY
TERRY
TOBY
TRACY
TRILBY
TYNE
WALLIS
WHITNEY
WYNN

We don't know any boys named Sue, but we sure do know a lot of girls named Alex. That seems to be the screenwriters' female moniker of choice these days. We've seen Jennifer Beals as Alex Owens in *Flashdance*, Jane Fonda as Alex Sternbergen in *The Morning After*, Debra Winger as Alex Barnes in *Black Widow*, and Cher as Alex Medford in *The Witches of Eastwick*. Most recently, Glenn Close (who was named Teddy in her last movie, *Jagged Edge*) joined the ranks, playing Alex Forrest in *Fatal Attraction*.

—*Premiere* magazine

FROM CLARISSA TO CARSON

You don't have to give up on a girl's name entirely because it's either too pink or too blue for your taste. Sometimes a slight twist can change a name from Feminissima to Feminine to No Frills to Boyish, or back again. Here are some names that, with a few changes, can span the degrees of femininity:

ADORA	ADRIANA
DORIA	ADRIENNE
DORIS	ADELE
DORIAN	ADDISON

ALEXANDR(I)A
ALEXA
ALEXIS
ALEX

ALYSSA
ALISON
ALICE
ALI

AURORA
FLORA
NORA
COREY

BELINDA
LINDA
LYNN
LINDSAY

CAROLINA
CAROLINE
CAROL
CAREY

CASSANDRA
CELESTE
CASS
CASEY

CECILY
CELIA

CEIL
CLEO

CLARISSA
CLARICE
CARLA
CARSON

ELISSA
ELIZA
ELLEN
ELLERY

EMMALINE
EMILY
EMMA
EMLYN

FRANCESCA
FRANCINE
FRANCES
FRANKIE

HYACINTH
VIOLET
ROSE
IVY

LOUELLA
LOUISA
LOUISE
LOU

MARIETTA	MELISSA
MARIEL	MELANIE
MARY	NELL
MERYL	MEL
MARILYN	TIFFANY
MARIA	T(H)ERESA
MARIAN	TESS
MALLORY	TERRY

FROM RAMBO TO SYLVESTER

Boys' names can be divided into four major gender categories. These are:

Macho: Names so hypermasculine they conjure up a frame from *Pumping Iron.*

Manly: The classic male names, used consistently over the centuries, suggesting traditional and clear-cut masculinity.

New manly: Boys' names that have burgeoned in popularity in the postfeminist era. While clearly masculine, these names nonetheless suggest a new, enlightened sort of man.

Wimpy: Sorry, Sylvester, but you're one of the group of male names with a weak image.

In this section, you'll find more details on what these categories mean, as well as lists of names that fall into each one.

Also here is a list of macho men who triumphed over their wimpy names, as well as a section on male names whose sexual image is shifting.

MACHO NAMES

If *Lethal Weapon* was your favorite movie and you're hoping for a little boy who'll strut through the world toting a plastic machine gun and pulling a toy tank, then one of these supermacho names is for you. But remember that even if your little Rod or Bart doesn't look or act like a bull on testosterone, he will always be measured against his name. Girls will giggle, boys will flex their muscles, and nursery-school teachers will wring their hands in anticipation.

Of course, a good many of these names have become jokes: Not many people would name their infant son Attila or Zoltan. But even the more reasonable names carry a lot of hypermasculine baggage. Giving your baby boy one of these macho names is like handing him a football, a hockey stick, and a baseball bat in the nursery and expecting him to play extremely well, or else.

Little Rod or Bart may rebel, the way some particularly well-known guys named Bruce, Arnold, and Sylvester have, but with less desirable consequences. For more on the contrary effect names can have on sexuality, see "Don't Pick a Fight with Bruce," page 172.

Macho names

ANGELO	HOLT
ATLAS	HUGO
AXEL	IGOR
BART	IVOR
BOONE	JOCK
BRAWLEY	KING
BROCK	KNOX
BRUNO	KNUTE
BRUTUS	MACK
BUBBA	MICK
BURR	OTTO
CLINT	PRIMO
CONAN	RAM
CORD	RAMBO
CURT	RIP
DALLAS	ROCCO
DAX	ROCK
DOLPH	ROCKY
DOMINIC	ROD
DUKE	SAMSON
FLINT	THOR
FORD	VITO
GUS	WOLF
HARLEY	ZOLTAN

MANLY NAMES

The names we call Manly have a Hallmark Father's Day card image: pipe, hunting dogs, golf clubs, the whole caboodle. They're the men's club of names, the Williams, Fredericks, and Josephs. If, in their proper form, some sound sort of, well, prissy, never fear; they come complete with Manly nicknames: Bill, Fred, Joe.

In terms of style, Manly names are on the upswing. With so many girls' names invading masculine turf—Whitney, Kyle, Alix, et al—boys' names are retreating to more exclusive ground. And many parents these days want their boys clearly to be boys, names and all.

Boys tend to fare well with these sturdy, classic names. No one ever gets teased for being called David, for instance, and no little Frank is ever mistaken for a girl on the basis of his name. The price you pay for this safety is that your son may not feel unique: There are relatively few classic boys' names and the selection is not all that inspired.

At the same time, the long craze for less traditional boys' names—the Jamies and Coreys, the Joshuas and Jasons of the last twenty years—freshens the sound of stalwarts like Henry and Fred. We may be moving back to the days when "every Tom, Dick, and Harry" was more than just a figure of speech.

Manly names

AL(L)AN/ALLEN	ANTHONY
ALBERT	ARTHUR
ALFRED	BERT/BURT
ANDREW	CARL

CHARLES	MARTIN
DANIEL	MICHAEL
DAVID	NEAL/NEIL
DONALD	NORMAN
DOUGLAS	PATRICK
EARL	PAUL
EDWARD	PETER
FRANK	PHIL(L)IP
FREDERICK	PRESTON
GEORGE	RALPH
GERALD	RAYMOND
GORDON	REX
HAROLD	RICHARD
HARRY	ROBERT
HARVEY	ROGER
HENRY	RONALD
HOWARD	ROY
HUGH	RUSSELL
IVAN	SAMUEL
JACK	STANLEY
JAMES	STEPHEN
JOHN	STUART/STEWART
JOSEPH	THEODORE
KENNETH	THOMAS
LAWRENCE	VICTOR
LEO	VINCENT
LEONARD	WALTER
LEWIS/LOUIS	WARREN
MARK	WILLIAM

NEW MANLY NAMES

The last decade has seen the emergence of a new breed of names: names that bespeak a transformed masculine ideal—sensitized, enlightened, liberated from the manacles of machismo. Names for guys with Alan Alda eyes (and maybe a Dustin Hoffman nose), guys who shop and cook and Pamper their babies. Guys who cry.

Some of these New Manly names have already worn out their welcome, while others remain in vogue. Although a certain percentage, like Jonathan and Joshua, have traditional roots, for the most part these names have been in wide use only since the publication of *The Feminine Mystique*. This is not to suggest that they are feminine names. Most are unmistakably male, but neither are they muscle-bound, far right, or radical.

This group of names is for little boys who may still prefer to play with trucks and build with blocks, but who probably also have at least one anatomically correct doll on their shelves.

It reflects the imagination of the first generation of parents not to rely on the inert pool of traditional male names for their sons. In the mid-sixties, names like Eric, Scott, and yes, Jason started appearing on the list of the top fifty names for boys; by 1982, Jason was number five and a flock of other Newly Manly names from Justin to Joshua to Jonathan had unseated such old standbys as Arthur, Frederick, and Peter.

One reason for the wild rise in popularity of these New Manly names is that it became unfashionable to name a boy after his father or any other family patriarch. Patriarchy itself was unfashionable. Each child was seen as an individual, to be given a fresh and creative start in life.

While many of these names are still popular, as a group they are not as stylish as they were even a few years ago. Most of the boys' names on the So Far In They're Out list can be found here. Exceptions are many of the surname names, as well as newcomers like Rex, Clay, and Duncan that buck the Tom, Dick, and Harry tradition but haven't been as overused as the Jason and Joshua group.

Does all this mean that New Men are out of style? Well, yes and no. Although today's New Man has dried his tears, he still dries the dishes, and this firmed-up masculine image is reflected in the naming of boy babies.

New manly names

AARON	BARNABY
ABEL	BARTHOLOMEW
ABNER	BEAU/BO
ADAM	BEN
AIDAN	BENEDICT
ALEC	BENJAMIN
ALEX	BEVAN
ALEXANDER	BLAINE
AMOS	BLAKE
ANGUS	BRADLEY
ANSON	BRADY
ARI	BRANDON
ARLO	BRENDAN
ASHER	BRETT
AUSTIN	BRODY
AVERY	BRYANT
BAILEY	CALE

CALEB	DONOVAN
CALVIN	DRAKE
CAMERON	DREW
CAMPBELL	DUNCAN
CAREY	DUSTIN
CARSON	DYLAN
CARTER	EBEN
CARVER	ELI
CASE	ELIA
CASEY	ELIAS
CHRISTIAN	ELIJAH
CHRISTOPHER	EL(L)IOT(T)
CLANCY	ELISHA
CLAY	ELLIS
CLEMENT	EMANUEL
CODY	EMMETT
COLIN	EPHRAIM
COREY	ERIC
CURTIS	ETHAN
DALE	EVAN
DALLAS	EVERETT
DALTON	EZRA
DAMIEN/DAMIAN	FABIAN
DANE	FORREST
DARCY	FOSTER
DASHIELL	GABRIEL
DAVIS	GARRETT
DENVER	GIDEON
DEREK	GRAHAM
DEVLIN	GRAY/GREY
DEVON	GREGORY
DIRK	GRIFFIN

HALE
HUBBELL
HUNTER
IAN
ISAAC
ISAIAH
JACKSON
JACOB
JAKE
JAMIE
JARED
JARRETT
JARVIS
JASON
JASPER
JED
JEDIDIAH
JEFFREY
JEREMIAH
JEREMIAS
JEREMY
JESSE
JODY
JON
JONAH
JONAS
JONATHAN
JORDAN
JOSH
JOSHUA
JOSIAH
JUD(D)

JUDE
JULIAN
JUSTIN
KAI
KEIL
KEIR
KELLY
KENT
KERRY
KIM
KIRK
KYLE
LANDON
LANE
LEMUEL
LEVI
LIAM
LINCOLN
LINUS
LIONEL
LOREN
LORNE
LUCAS
LUCIAN
LUCIUS
LUKE
MACKENZIE
MALACHI/
    MALACHY
MALCOLM
MARC
MARCO

MARCUS	ROLLO
MASON	RORY
MATTHEW	ROSS
MATTHIAS	ROWAN
MAX	RUFUS
MAXFIELD	RUPERT
MAXWELL	RYAN
MICAH	SAM
MILO	SAUL
MORGAN	SAWYER
MOSES	SEAN/SHAWN
NATHAN	SEBASTIAN
NATHANIEL	SETH
NED	SHANE
NICHOLAS	SILAS
NOAH	SIMON
NOEL	SOLOMON
NOLAN	TAYLOR
OLIVER	THADDEUS
OMAR	THEO
OTIS	TIMOTHY
OWEN	TOBIAH
QUENTIN	TOBIAS
QUINN	TRACY
RAPHAEL	TRAVIS
REDMOND	TREVOR
REED	TRISTAN
RENO	TYLER
REO	WALKER
REUBEN	WEBB
RILEY	WILEY/WYLIE
ROBINSON	WILL

WYATT	ZACK/ZAK
WYNN	ZANE
YALE	ZED
ZACHARIAH/S	ZEKE
ZACHARY	

WIMPY NAMES

No matter how sensitive you want your son to be, you surely don't want to brand him as a wimp. You don't want to give him a name that will get him picked last for every team, shunned in every game of spin the bottle, turned down for every blind date.

Unfair as it may seem, the Selwyns and Percys and Egberts of this world tend to meet one of two terrible fates. Either they knuckle under to their names, and *become* Selwyns or Percys or Egberts; or they bust their gonads proving that, despite the wimpy label, they're really Rods or Brunos or Rambos.

We have been conservative in devising this list. We have avoided borderline wimpy names, and concentrated on the hard (soft?) core group. What relegates a name to terminal wimpdom?

Once-ambisexual names now used almost exclusively for girls qualify: Lynn or Courtney, for example. A feminine sound, like the sibilant Percy or Sylvester, can push a name into the wimp category. And any name ending in "-bert" (Hubert, Egbert, Wilbert) or "-ville" (Melville, Orville) or "-wyn/vin" (Selwyn, Melvin) almost automatically triggers a wimp response in the modern ear.

This brings up a salient point for any of you out there with decidedly nonwimpy uncles or fathers named Bernard or Melvin. Perceptions of wimpiness tend to change over generations. As Russell Baker points out (see page 173), Jason was once one of the biggest wimp names going. And a name that seems perfectly substantial for a fifty-year-old man can suddenly go limp when applied to a newborn baby of today.

Obviously, this list is intended more as a warning than a guidepost. If you're determined to go ahead with one of these names, maybe you should be prepared to spend your old age introducing Percy as "My son, the butterfly collector" or "My son, the mercenary guerrilla." Tough choice, eh?

Wimpy names

AINSLEY	CECIL
ALGERNON	CEDRIC
ALOYSIUS	CHARLTON
ALVIN	CLARENCE
AMBERT	CONWAY
ARNOLD	CORNELIUS
BEAUREGARD	COURTNEY
BENTLEY	CYRIL
BERNARD	DABNEY
BERTRAM	DELMORE
BLAIR	DEWEY
BROOKE	DURWOOD
BROOKS	DWIGHT
BRUCE	EDGAR
BURTON	EGBERT
CARLTON	ELBERT
CARROLL	ELLSWORTH

ELMER	MARMADUKE
ELROY	MARVIN
EUGENE	MAURICE
FARLEY	MAYNARD
FERDINAND	MELVILLE
FLOYD	MELVIN
FRANCIS	MERLE
GALE	MERLIN
GAYLORD	MERTON
GOMER	MERVYN
HARLAN	MILTON
HARMON	MONROE
HERBERT	MORTIMER
HERMAN	MURRAY
HORACE	MYRON
HUBERT	NORBERT
HUMPHREY	ORVILLE
HYMAN	OSBERT
IRA	OSWALD
IRVING	PERCIVAL
IRWIN	PERCY
JULIUS	REGINALD
KERWIN	RODNEY
LANCE	SANFORD
LEON	SELWYN
LESLIE	SEYMOUR
LESTER	SHELDON
LYNDON	SHERMAN
LYNN	SHERWOOD
MANFRED	SYLVESTER
MARION	THURMAN
MARLON	VANCE

VERNON   WILBERT
VIRGIL   WILBUR
WENDELL   WILFRED
WESLEY

Don't Pick a Fight with Bruce

A wimpy name does not necessarily a wimpy boy make. In fact, the world is full of Bruces, Arnolds, and Sylvesters we wouldn't want to meet in a dark alley. Maybe these guys became supermacho in reaction to their anemic names, or maybe they would have overdeveloped biceps even if their names were Brawley or Flint. Here, a list of famous tough guys with anything but tough names.

ARNOLD Schwarzenegger
BROOKS Robinson
BRUCE Jenner
BRUCE Lee
BRUCE Springsteen
BRUCE Weitz
CARLTON Fisk
CARROLL O'Connor
CECIL Cooper
CHARLTON Heston
CLARENCE Clemons
DWIGHT Gooden
ELROY Hirsch
ELVIS Presley
ERNEST Borgnine
ERNEST Hemingway
EVANDER Holyfield
FRAN Tarkenton
GALE Sayers
GAYLORD Perry
JULIUS Erving
HARMON Killebrew
HERSCHEL Walker

HUMPHREY Bogart	MEL Gibson
LEON Spinks	MERLE Haggard
LYNDON Johnson	MERLIN Olsen
LYNN Swann	OREL Herscheiser
MARION Motley	REGGIE Jackson
MARLON Brando	SYLVESTER Stallone
MARVIN Hagler	THURMAN Munson

What Jason Was

When I was a child, only the most sadistic parents named their children Jason. . . . Like Percy and Horace, Jasons existed only to be beaten in the schoolyard by classmates named Spike and Butch.

—Russell Baker, "A Name for All Seasons," Sunday Observer, *The New York Times*

BEACH BOYS

In the late fifties and early sixties, no names were cooler than Gary, Glenn, and Greg. They were the personification of surfer machismo. Now, however, these Beach Boy names have lost their muscle. They are too old to be new men, too young to be manly, too soft to be macho, and too firm to be truly wimpy. This group of masculine nomads includes:

BRAD	GLENN
BRIAN	GREG
CHAD	KEITH
CRAIG	KEVIN
DARREN	RICK
DARRYL	SCOTT
DEAN	TODD
DENNIS	TROY
DUANE/DWAYNE	WAYNE
GARY	

At five, Marlon had an angelic face and a pugnacious nature, developed as a defense against neighborhood bullies who taunted him about his fancy-sounding name.

—*The Star*, excerpted from *Brando: A Biography in Photographs*, by Christopher Nickens

"Do they mean Bruce Springsteen? Bruce Willis? Bruce really seems to be the in name these days."

—Bruce Boxleitner on TV talk show when shown two girls wearing I Love Bruce buttons

AMBISEXUAL NAMES

The trend over the past twenty years has increasingly been to bestow ambisexual names upon girls rather than boys. And once a name moves from the male province into the female, there's usually no going back.

There have been a number of transsexual shifts in the history of nomenclature. Alice, Anne, Crystal, Emma, Esmé, Evelyn, Florence, Jocelyn, Kimberly, Lucy, and Maud all were originally male names. Christian was a feminine name in the Middle Ages, as was Douglas in the seventeenth century and Clarence in the eighteenth. A king of East Anglia in the seventh century was named Anna.

In the sixties, it was more usual to find a boy with an ambisexual name than it is now. The big trend in that consciousness-raising time was toward cute nicknames that sounded just as right for boys as for girls: Jody, Toby, Jamie. This continued in the seventies with ambisexual nicknames that were short for more sexually distinct proper names. There were plenty of Chrises, Nickys, and Alexes around, but on their birth certificates they were Christopher or Christine, Nicholas or Nicole, Alexander or Alexandra.

More recently we've moved back to ambisexual proper names without nicknames, but, as detailed in the Androgynous Executive list in the What's Hot section, these are used more and more for girls rather than boys. While a carriage bearing an Alexis, Blair, or Jordan may still hold a boy, it's more likely that the blanket in it will be pink and the baby will be female.

In the vanguard of style, parents are even considering traditionally masculine names for their daughters. One couple we know—a television producer and a theatrical lawyer—said that if their child was a girl, they would name her George. Fortunately, they had a boy.

We've arranged the following list of Ambisexual names from those that are at the moment used almost exclusively for girls to those used primarily for boys. When a name had variant spellings for boys and girls, we've included both, but with nickname names like Ricky and Terry, we've listed only the ambi y ending.

This list can be a help in determining the current gender standing of a name. But, be warned: We predict that by the turn of the next century many of the names in the 50 percent range will have moved into the feminine dominion, and that names like Jordan and Perry and Daryl may well be considered about as appropriate for a boy as, say, Sue.

90 percent feminine

ALLIE/ALLY
ANDREA

CAROL (f);
CARROLL (m)

CHRISTIE/CHRISTY	LACEY
CLAIRE (f); CLARE	LAURIE
(f,m)	LESLIE/LESLEY
COURTNEY	LYNN
EVELYN	MARIAN/MARION
GAIL (f); GALE (f,m)	PA(I)GE
HA(Y)LEY	PATSY
HIL(L)ARY	SHANNON
JOYCE	STACY
KAY	TRACY

75 percent feminine

ALEXIS	KIT
ASHLEY	LAUREN (f); LOREN
BLAIR	(f,m)
BROOKE	LINDSAY/LINDSEY
BRYN	MALLORY
DANA	MEREDITH
JAN	MERRILL
KELLY	ROBIN
KELSEY	SACHA/SASHA
KERRY	SHELL(E)Y
KIM	WHITNEY

50/50

ALEX	ANGEL
ALI	BO

BRETT
CAREY
CASEY
CASS
CHRIS
COREY
DALE
DARCY
DEVON
DORIAN
EVAN
FRANCES (f);
  FRANCIS (m)
GERRY (f,m); JERRY
  (f,m)
HOLLIS
JAMIE
JEAN (f); GENE (f,m)
JESS(I)E
JODY

JORDAN
KAI
LANE
LEE (f,m); LEIGH (f)
MACKENZIE
MICKEY
MORGAN
NICKY
PAT
PAYTON
RICKY
SHAWN (f,m);
  SEAN (m)
STORM
SYDNEY (f,m);
  SIDNEY (m)
TERRY
TOBY
WALLIS (f,m);
  WALLACE (m)

75 percent male

BAILEY
BLAKE
CAMERON
DAKOTA
DARIN/DARREN
DAR(R)YL
DREW
DYLAN

ELLERY
EMLYN
KEIL
KIRBY
KYLE
NEVADA
NOEL (m,f); NOELLE (f)
NORRIS

PALMER
PARKER
PERRY
PORTER
QUINN
RANDY
RAY (m,f); RAE (f)
REED
REGAN
RORY
SAM

SCHUYLER
SHELBY
SIERRA
SLOAN
TAYLOR
TYLER
VALENTINE
WALKER
WYNN
YAEL

90 percent masculine

ADDISON
AIDAN
AL(L)AN/ALLEN (m);
  ALLYN (m,f)
BROWN
CHRISTOPHER
CLAUDE
DALLAS
GARY

GEORGE
GLENN
MEL
MICHAEL
SETH
SHANE
ZANE

No Boys Named Maria

In 1932, the Supreme Court of Czechoslovakia ruled that Maria would no longer be allowed as a name for male children. The tribunal decided that a given name must clearly denote an individual's sex.

"By the time Jamie goes to college, it's probably going to cost about $29,000 a year. Either I'd better make some smart decisions or else she'd better learn to play football."

—Citibank TV commercial

TRADITION

"Hakeem?" "Here." "Liam?" "Here." "Sarita?" "Here." Attendance-taking time at any self-respecting preschool these days will tell you that tradition as an influence on naming is back with a vengeance.

You, like many parents, may be looking into your own familial history—canvassing the names of grandparents, great-aunts, and uncles—to come up with a name for your child that reflects your cultural heritage. You may be considering a family surname for your baby's middle or even first name, whether your child is a boy or a girl. And if a suitable name can't be plucked from your own family tree, you may find yourself wandering into other orchards in search of a seasoned name, a name with substance.

To give you a perspective on the past, we offer here a history of this century's naming trends, the fashions and fads that typified each decade. Also here is a guide to nicknames: the rise and fall in popularity of a range of abbreviated forms, including some no longer used versions—Daisy for Margaret, for example, or Hobbin for Robert—you may find worth consideration.

You may want to incorporate tradition in your child's name by choosing one that reflects your ethnic heritage. Let's say you're Irish, and you'd like to explore options beyond the obvious Shannon, Kevin, and cousins. In one section here you'll learn that Brett, Tracy, Darren, and Troy, among others, would all be authentically Irish choices, even though you may have believed otherwise. Another chapter will give you some exotic names—how do Annora, Juno, Curran, or Eamon strike you?—popular in Ireland but rarely heard here, along with similar lists for other cultural backgrounds, from Hebrew to Italian to Hungarian. And if you're looking for a name to reflect black heritage, included here are lists of Arabic and African names.

If your hope is to come up with a name that connects to the religious traditions of your family, you may want to consult the list of unexpected saints' names—and take this book to the baptism to convince the priest there really is a Saint Benno. Also here is a guide to Jewish naming traditions, including examples of how the first-initial practice and secular trends have combined to bring naming patterns full circle.

Our focus on tradition narrows in the chapter called Family Ties. Are you and your spouse wrestling over name choices? Here's why, plus tips to help you come to a compatible decision. If you're thinking of making your son a junior, you'll find the pros and cons here. Also here is a guide to sibling names—for first-time parents, too! And finally, we offer a primer on living with your ultimate choice of name.

Here, then, to Tradition, the fourth important factor in choosing the right name for your child.

AMERICAN NOMENCLATURE

TRADITION IN PROGRESS

There are two currents of tradition in American names.

One is really an English tradition, names brought over by the Pilgrims and handed down from generation to generation, from century to century. Mary, Ann, Catherine, and Elizabeth; John, James, Charles, Joseph, Robert, William, and Edward were as well used here in 1750 as they were in 1900 and as they are today, but are no more uniquely American than, say, an *Oxford Dictionary*.

A naming tradition America could call its own didn't really blossom until 1920. By that time, when our parents' parents bobbed their hair and shaved their mustaches, put in a phone, and searched for modern baby names, there were places to look: at the marquee of the new movie theatre down the block, to the voices on the radio now dominating the living room, or at the neighbors who just arrived from County Cork.

American tradition is one part history and three parts ex-
perimentation, fashion, and progress—with a strong dash of
folly. To get a true picture, you have to consider chili dogs
along with apple pie, Groundhog Day as well as the Fourth
of July, Mickey along with Michael.

Here, a look at the naming tradition we've just begun to
create.

The 64 Percent Solution

It has been estimated that in fourteenth-century
England 64 percent of all male children were
given one of the following five names:

HENRY
JOHN
ROBERT
WILLIAM
RICHARD

Today, by contrast, roughly the same propor-
tion of boys receive names ranked in the top
fifty.

The 1920s and 1930s: Freckles, France, and Hollywood

The hottest trend in the 1920s and early 1930s was freckle-faced names for girls and boys, Our Gang comedy names that came complete with button noses, big ears, and overbites. A lot of these were nicknames for perennial favorites—Billy or Willie for William, for example, or Margie, Maggie, and Peggy for Margaret—but others were proper names you just don't hear much anymore:

G I R L S

BETSY	PATSY
BINNIE	PEGGY
DOLLY	PENNY
GWEN	POLLY
KATHLEEN	SALLY
KITTY	TRUDY
MARY ANN	WINNIE

B O Y S

BARNEY	FRANKLIN
CALVIN	HAL
CHESTER	HOMER
CLEM	MICKEY
DEXTER	NED
ELMER	WILBUR
EUGENE	WILLIS

At the same time, several names, often those popularized by stars, were new arrivals on the best-seller list. For girls: Alice,

Barbara, Betty, Jean, Marion, Myrna, Patricia, Shirley, and Virginia; for boys, Arthur, Clarence, Donald, Harry, Henry, Richard, and Thomas.

Other female fads for the period included names of the months (April, May, and June); names ending in the letter *s* (Phyllis, Frances, Doris, Lois, Iris); and names ending in -*een* or -*ine*—Irish ones like Eileen, Maureen, Pegeen, Noreen, Kathleen, and Colleen, or more Gallic specimens like Jacqueline, Maxine, Arlene, Nadine, Pauline, and Marlene, which followed in the wake of such earlier favorites as Irene, Geraldine, and Josephine. Even more fashionably French were Annette, Claudette, Paulette, Georgette, Jeanette, and Nanette, not to mention Rochelle, Estelle, and Isabel.

Diamond-Studded Names

What were the most glittery names of 1927? Or at least what did the copywriters of the Sears, Roebuck catalog of that year think would appear as such to their constituency when they decided to give girls' names to the various models of "Genuine Brilliant Diamond Rings"?
They were:

ABBIE	BEULAH
ALICE	CLARICE
ANGELA	ELAINE
ANNA MAY	ELEANOR
ANNETTE	FLORENCE
BETTY JANE	GENEVIEVE

HONORA	MARILYN
INEZ	MILDRED
IRENE	MINERVA
JANET	PAULINE
KATHRYN	RUTH
LORRAINE MAY	VIOLA
LYDIA	

The 1930s and 1940s: Hi Mom! Hi Dad! I'm home!

During the mid-thirties through the forties, names like Dorothy, Anne, Shirley, Ruth, George, Frank, Edward, and Clarence fell off the top ten, to be replaced by Carol, Judith, Joan, Linda, Ronald, and David. Other new names were moving in as well—"sophisticated" names for kids whose parents envisioned them triumphing over the Depression and growing up to use cigarette holders, wear glamorous evening clothes, and live in Hollywood-inspired mansions. Television was still in its infancy, so no one could foresee that these would become the sitcom mom and dad names of the next generation:

G I R L S

ANITA	DEBORAH
ARLENE	DIANE
AUDREY	ELAINE
BEVERLY	ELLEN
BRENDA	GAIL
CYNTHIA	JANET

JOANNE
LORRAINE
LYNN
MARILYN
MARJORIE
NANCY
NATALIE

PAMELA
RENÉE
ROBERTA
SANDRA
SHEILA
SUSAN

B O Y S

AL(L)AN/ALLEN
BARRY
CHRISTOPHER
EL(L)IOT(T)
EUGENE
GERALD
HAROLD
HARVEY
HOWARD
IRA
JOEL
LAWRENCE
MARTIN
MICHAEL

MITCHELL
NEIL/NEAL
NORMAN
PAUL
PETER
PHIL(L)IP
ROGER
ROY
RUSSELL
STANLEY
STEPHEN
VINCENT
WALTER

The 1950s: Ranch houses and barbeques

The postwar baby boom moving into the fifties spawned a whole new generation of cuter, younger, glossier names, names for kids who would play with Tiny Tears dolls and watch Captain Kangaroo, oblivious to the hard times just past. These names reflected a collective lust for a new way of life, the good life in the suburbs. Linda jumped from number ten to number one in popularity and Karen appeared out of nowhere to take the tenth spot. Michael, a Biblical name that had been out of favor for over a hundred years, catapulted to number two. Other newly popular names in the fifties, many of which remained in vogue through the Kennedy administration, were:

G I R L S

AMY	JANICE
CHARLENE	JULIE
CHERYL	LISA
CHRISTINE	MICHELLE
DARLENE	ROBIN
DENISE	SHARON
DONNA	TERRY
HEIDI	TINA
HOLLY	WENDY

B O Y S

ANDREW	ERIC
ANTHONY	GARY
BRIAN	GREGORY
BRUCE	JEFFREY
CRAIG	KENNETH
DEAN	KEVIN
DENNIS	LEE
DOUGLAS	MARK

MATTHEW	TERRY
PATRICK	TIMOTHY
SCOTT	TODD

The 1960s: Do your own thing

In the sixties and early seventies, as men grew their hair to their shoulders and women abandoned their bras, Karens and Craigs gave way to Caryns and Chastitys, Kellys and Clouds. In deference to the new credo of "do your own thing," new names were invented, familiar forms of old names became perfectly acceptable, and the spelling of traditional names became a contest of creativity. The ultimate trendy name of the sexually liberated sixties and early seventies was actually a relaxed nickname name, preferably ambi-gender. We saw a lot of the following:

CANDY	MANDY
CARRIE/CAREY	MARCY
CASEY	MARNIE
CINDY	MINDY
COREY	RICKI/RICKY
JAMIE	SHARI
JESSIE/JESSE	SHELL(E)Y
JODY	SHERRY
JONI/JON	STACY
KELLY	TAMMY
KERRY	TAWNY
KIM	TRACY
LORI	

Even more revolutionary were such invented hippie names as:

AMERICA	PEACE
ASIA	PHOENIX
BREEZE	RAIN
CHE	RAINBOW
CHINA	REBEL
CLOUD	RIVER
DAKOTA	SEASON
DUNE	SENECA
ECHO	SEQUOIAH
FOREST	SIERRA
FREE	SKY
GYPSY	SPRING
HARMONY	STAR
LEAF	STARSHINE
LIBERTY	SUMMER
LIGHT	SUNSHINE
LOVE	TRUE
MORNING	WELCOME
OCEAN	WILLOW

The Names, They Are A-Changing

Now that lovebeads and elephant bells are nostalgia items, many of the flower children's children are trading in their hippie names for more mainstream ones. Zowie Bowie, for instance, son of David Bowie, now calls himself Joey. Free, born to David Carradine and Barbara Hershey when she was calling herself Barbara Seagull, has changed his name to Tom. And Susan St. James, who named her first two children Harmony and Sunshine, called her sons born in the eighties Charlie and William.

As the children born in the sixties and early seventies come of age, however, we'll be hearing more from those who are standing by the names given them by their idealistic parents. One already notable example is River Phoenix, who came to prominence in the 1986 film, *Stand by Me*. River's sisters are named Rainbow, Liberty, and Summer Joy, and his brother is named Leaf. The father of the Phoenix family is named—what else?—John.

The 1970s: Ahead to the past

The mid-seventies saw the beginnings of a reawakening of patriotism, but this tentative romance was with a pre-Watergate, pre-Vietnam, pre-Bomb, pre-Depression, pre-Industrial Revolution America—way back to the old West. Fifty years after the birth of a uniquely American naming tradition, we finally summoned the confidence to delve back into our country's own past, launching a nation of little urban cowboys and their pioneer-women sisters named:

G I R L S

AMY	JESSIE
ANNIE	KATIE
BECKY	MAGGIE
JENNY	MOLLY

B O Y S

ETHAN	JOSH
JASON	LUKE
JED	SHANE
JESSE	ZANE

Also, Biblical names like Aaron, Adam, Benjamin, Jacob, Jonathan, Rachel, Rebecca, Sarah, and Samuel were born again, even if the parents choosing them weren't.

Those who couldn't or didn't want to reach back to the frontier or the Bible for their roots looked to their own or other people's ethnic backgrounds for inspiration (see Roots, page 227). Names derived from the Irish or French became particularly popular, even for parents who weren't Irish or French. Thus were born thousands of Brians, Dylans, Erins, Kellys, Kevins, Megans, Ryans, Seans, Shannons, and Taras. For girls, the French twist was the rage, with names such as Danielle, Michelle (given a big boost by the Beatles song), and Nicole.

Other little girls were liberated from female stereotypes with names previously reserved for effete upper-class gentle-men: Ashley, Blake, Brooke, Courtney, Kimberly, Lindsay, and Whitney. Similar in tone, although they were always girls' names, are Hayley (as in Mills) and Tiffany (yes: a Charlie's Angel).

At the opposite end of the scale is a group of girls' names as purely feminine as a lavender sachet. These are the wildly popular Victorian valentine names, which include Alexandra, Alyssa (in all its variant spellings), Amanda, Jennifer, Jessica, Samantha, Melissa, Vanessa, and Victoria. Their male counterparts are Alexander, Brett, Justin, and Nicholas.

Today, while many of the names that became popular in the 1970s are still widely used, their fashion status is fading. But their legacy is important: They reflect renewed ties with tradition, the rejuvenation of forgotten classics, a closer bond between names and ethnic or religious heritage. These issues are important to many of today's parents, whose name choices will influence the American traditions of tomorrow.

THE HUNDRED-YEAR CYCLE

When was the last time that names like Alexander, Benjamin, Amanda, and Gregory were in vogue? A startling number of the names that sound fresh and appealing to us today were favored by the new parents of a hundred years ago. Appearing in the top-fifty lists a century ago were:

G I R L S

ANNIE	JENNIE
CARRIE	KATHERINE
CHARLOTTE	LAURA
ELIZABETH	LILLIE
EMILY	LUCY

REBECCA   SOPHIA
SARA(H)

B O Y S

ALEXANDER	HENRY
ANDREW	JACOB
BENJAMIN	JAMES
CHARLES	JOHN
DAVID	SAMUEL
EDWARD	WILLIAM
HARRY	

Other names that didn't make the top fifty but were in fashion a hundred years ago, and are back in style now, include:

G I R L S

AMANDA	LOUISE
CHRISTINA	MADELINE
CLAIRE	MAGGIE
DAISY	OLIVIA
JULIA	POLLY
LEAH	RACHEL

B O Y S

AARON	GREGORY
ADAM	JESSE
ANTHONY	JONAH
BEN	JONATHAN
ERIC	JOSHUA

LUKE	PATRICK
MAX	SETH
NATHAN	TIMOTHY
NOAH	

CATHERINE, KATHARINE, AND KATHRYNNE

You've always loved the name Catherine. But you want your Catherine to be unique; different from all others in the world, so you decide to spell it Kathrynne.

You see the first signs of trouble while still in the hospital, where you are asked to spell the name eleven times. This is followed by similar requests from friends, parents, in-laws, aunts, and cousins, who nevertheless send cards and little pink panda bears addressed to Katharine, Katherine, Kathryn, Kathrinne, and Kathy Lynn.

Creative naming was one of the least felicitous minirevolutions to take place during the Age of Aquarius, when suddenly there was a nonaggressive army of Alicias, Alishas, Alysias, Alisas, Alyssas, Elissas, Elyssas, Ilysas, and Ilyssas peacefully coexisting in the park with Arons, Jaysens, Kristoffers, and Jimis.

While the use of unconventional spellings if no longer epidemic, the practice continues. Recent aberrations noted on birth announcements have included Kassie, Kacie, Kaitlin, Crystine, Holli, Malissa, Megean, Ryann, Jayme, and Jaimie.

Many of these children will grow up surrounded by people who think they don't know how to spell their own names, or that their parents (this means you) were simply ignorant.

Poor Megean will have to spend countless hours explaining whether her name rhymes with Pegeen, Regan, or leg in, and many more hours correcting all the people who spell her name wrong by spelling it right.

A different issue arises when a name has bona fide variant spellings, each of which is widely used and accepted. Once again, Catherine is a case in point: the C spelling is originally French and commonly used in Britain; Katherine is the most common form in the United States and Canada; Katharine is derived from the name's Roman version and also well used here; and Kathryn is a spelling used since the turn of the century and popularized in the 1940s by the actress Kathryn (b. Zelma) Grayson.

Other names with more than one well-accepted spelling include Ann/Anne, Sara/Sarah, Alison/Allison, Stuart/Stewart, Teresa/Theresa, Alan/Allan/Allen, Geoffrey/Jeffrey, Lee/Leigh, Philip/Phillip, and Stephen/Steven.

While all these names are pronounced the same whatever the spelling, which form you choose seems to alter the name in subtle ways. Katherine, for instance, seems somewhat hipper than Catherine, which has a more feminine and gently old-fashioned connotation. Ann seems more no-nonsense than Anne, Leigh more delicate than Lee, Geoffrey more buttoned-up than Jeffrey.

When there is more than one correct spelling of a name, let your own feelings on the image each conjures up be your guide. Catherine, Katherine, Katharine, and Kathryn are all perfectly correct choices, and all a far sight better than (please don't) Kathrynne.

> I kept wishing for some poor people, some important characters much older, or younger, than these nummies, someone whose name weren't Garrett, or Gaye, or Kyle, or Renée, or Drew.
>
> —Thomas R. Edwards, review of *Where You'll Find Me and Other Stories* by Ann Beattie, *The New York Times* Book Review

> Twenty years ago, when I was born, my mother named me Jennifer Lyn. I don't think she anticipated the thousands of Jennifers who would flourish. I have met 25 other Jennifers; all with the middle name of either Lyn or Ann. Two of my three best friends are Jennifers. Pet names keep us straight: Jen, Little J, Jenny. I wouldn't change my name for the world.
>
> —Letter to the editor from Jennifer Lyn Caron, *Elle*

WHY JENNIFER AND JASON?

How did Jennifer and Jason become popular to the point of infamy?

Jennifer, consistently the number-one name in most states in the seventies and eighties, was an overnight success largely inspired by the doomed heroine Jenny in *Love Story*. But while the book—and later the movie—may have launched the name, a perfect fit with the spirit of the times sustained it.

Jennifer was a name with something for almost everyone. For down-home, back-to-the-land types, it had the cowgirlish nickname Jenny. Jenny, by itself, was also a Grandma and Grandpa name (foreshadowing today's popularity of Max, Sam, et al) shared by grandmas who hailed from places as diverse as Minsk and Mayo. And Jennifer in its full glory had a romantically feminine Victorian flavor as well as a euphonic, air-brushed quality—both in vogue in the seventies.

Jason, on the other hand, never quite made it to number one: More traditional boys' names like Michael and Christopher claimed that honor. But Jason is the quintessential trendy boy's name of the seventies—newfangled but old-fashioned, with roots in both the Old West and the New Testament. Again, many different types of parents—from Jews to born-again Christians, from Ms. magazine readers to Clint Eastwood fans—could, and did, find a reason to name their sons Jason.

Jason's and even Jennifer's star is on the wane now. While Jennifer is a name that still has mass appeal, many parents are turning away from it because of the sheer volume of little Jennifers. But the names they're favoring instead—notably Ashley, Amanda, and Jessica—have such a similar flavor that they seem like consolation prizes. Jason is suffering from a more rapid decline, losing out to classic upstarts like Andrew, Daniel, and Nicholas.

A GRAND OLD NAME

For three centuries, from the days when Mary was dressed in sober gowns of Puritan gray, to the days when she wore a bustle, to the days when she bobbed her hair, her name was always the most popular. The Greek and New Testament version of the Hebrew Miriam, Mary was considered too holy for mortal use until the twelfth century; by the sixteenth, it had become the most frequently used girl's name, a position it held until 1950.

That year, Linda made headline news by toppling Mary from the number-one spot. Mary continued on a downward slide, dropping to number fifteen in 1970 and thirty-four in 1983. Even the current resurgence in classic names has not boosted Mary back into favor.

The problem may be that Mary has become more of an icon than a name. Besides its association with the Blessed Virgin, it has a persistently ethnic ring and a fade-into-the-woodwork quality. Three hundred years of popularity have turned it into a generic term.

The name Mary remains fascinating, however, because of all the ways it has been used and the variations it has spawned. Some Catholic parents, for instance, use it as a token first name, followed by a sprightlier middle name by which their child is known. All four female members of the Fisher quintuplets, born in 1963, were named Mary: Mary Ann, Mary Magdalene, Mary Catherine, and Mary Margaret. And two of Robert and Ethel Kennedy's four daughters are named Mary—Mary Courtney and Mary Kerry—but called only by their middle names. The idea is that, since a Catholic child must carry a saint's name, Mary is sanctified enough to cover all bases, including a "heathen" middle name.

More often, when Mary is linked with another name, both are used. This "Mary-plus" trend reached its height in the 1940s and continued into the fifties, with variations ranging from the sedate Mary Ann and Mary Frances to the hep Mary Sue and Mary Jo to the oh-so-cute twins named Mary Pride and, yes, Mary Joy.

If the Mary-plus fad had (thankfully) gone the way of poodle skirts, derivations of the name Mary have become somewhat more common in this country. Those used here include:

MARA	MARINA
MARIA	MARIS
MARIAH	MARIS(S)A
MARIAN/MARION	MARLA
MARIAN(N)A	MARLENE
MARIANNE	MARLO
MARIBEL	MARYA
MARIE	MAURA
MARIEL	MAUREEN
MARIETTA	MAY
MARIETTE	MERRY
MARILEE ·	MIA
MARILYN	MOLLY
MARIN	

The name Mary has no fewer foreign variations, which include the Irish Maire and Moira, the French Manette, the British Marigold, and—back to the source—the Hebrew Marilla.

VARIATIONS ON A THEME

When we were growing up, you weren't cool if you didn't have a nickname. Patti, Judy, Billy, and Bobby would rather have traded in their Beatle boots than be known to the world as Patricia, Judith, William, and Robert. The epitome of keen was to have a name that nobody could formalize when they were mad at you, a name that was a nickname: Jamie, Jody, Ricki.

President Carter changed all that. When he sighed in as Jimmy in 1976, many people felt buoyed by the symbolism: He was a common man, leader of a nation of Toms and Daves, Kathys and Debbies. Later, the general sentiment was that a Jimmy wasn't up to the job: We needed a James to take us into the eighties. We elected Ronald—Ronnie only to his intimates and his enemies—Reagan and readopted the names on our own birth certificates, becoming Jameses and Deborahs and Richards ourselves.

Now, we're also favoring unabbreviated forms for our children: Today's little Elizabeth is more likely to lisp through all four syllables of her name than to introduce herself as Beth, Betsy, Libby, Lizzie, or any of the other possibilities.

This no-nickname trend has intensified what has long been a concern for parents: how to prevent other people from using the wrong—or any—nickname. Some parents solve this dilemma by choosing a name with no common diminutive: Claire, for example, or Ethan. Others may avoid a name they like because it has a nickname they don't care for. Two sets of parents we know decided against Susannah because they couldn't bear Susie or Sue; another couple who wanted to name their son Edward and call him Ned got cold feet at the possibility of raising an Eddie.

Nicknaming began in medieval England, where there were so few Christian names in general usage that it was not unusual for two children in a family to have the same name. The only way to distinguish the two Jameses was for one to be Jamey, the other Jem.

Many proper names that have remained in common use since that time have accumulated a procession of nicknames that reflect changing styles. Some of these nicknames were popular at one point and then died out: Tetty for Elizabeth, Sukey for Susan, and Hob for Robert, for example. Others have regularly moved in and out of fashion.

Here, with the range of nicknames used over time—arranged in order from the earliest to the most recent favorites—are some examples:

ELIZABETH

BESS	BETTY
ELIZA	BETTE
BET	BETSY
TETTY	LISA
TETSY	LIZ
LIZZIE	LIZA
BETH	BETH
BESSIE	LIZZY
LIBBY	BESS

CATHERINE/KATHERINE

KITTY	KITTY
KATE	
CAT	

CATHY/KATHY   CASSY
KAY   KIT
     KATIE
     KATE

M A R G A R E T

DAISY   PEG
MAISIE   MARGE
MAGGIE   MARGIE
MAG   MARGY
MEG   MAGGIE
MADGE   MEG
PEGGY

M A R Y

MAL   MINNIE
MALLY   MAMIE
MOLL   MAME
MOLLY   MITZI
POLLY   MIMI
MAY

P A T R I C I A

PAT   PATTY
PATTY   PATTI
PATSY   TRICIA
     TRISH

LAURA

LOLLY
LOW
LOR

LAURIE
LORI

BARBARA

BAB
BABBY
BABS

BOBBIE/BOBBY
BARB
BARBIE

WILLIAM

WILL
WILLY
WILLIE
BILL

BILLY
WILLIE
WILL

ROBERT

ROB
HOB
NOB
DOB
DOBBIN
ROBIN

BERT
BOB
BOBBY
ROBBIE
ROB

EDWARD

NED	EDDY
TED	ED
EDDIE	NED
TEDDY	

RICHARD

RICH	DICK
HITCH	RICHIE
RICK	RICK
HICK	RICKY

The ultimate fate of many of these series of nicknames is that those most widely used became names in their own right. Today, for instance, Molly and Kate are heard as often as their progenitors, Mary and Katherine. Other nicknames that have spun off into proper names bear little or no connection to their original forms. Nancy was once a nickname for Anne, for example, as was Sally for Sarah and Lisa for Elizabeth.

The Pete Pan Syndrome

A good case against calling your child by any kind of nickname can be found in the results of a study headed by Von Leirer, a psychologist at Human Cognition Research in Stanford, Cal-

ifornia. Students were asked to judge six ficti-
tious people—two with formal names (like Peter), two with familiar ones (Pete), and two with
"adolescent" nicknames (Petey). The Peters
were rated as more conscientious, more emo-
tionally stable, and more cultivated than the
Petes and Peteys.

THE KOSHER CURVE

In general, except for the comparatively few people who are using Hebrew names for their children, there is no such thing as a "Jewish" first name anymore. The days when Molly Goldberg sticking her head out of her Bronx tenement window and calling down to her son Sammy meant immediate ethnic identification are long gone. These days, Sam's last name could just as readily be Gallagher and Mrs. Goldberg's son could be named Sean.

When today's Samuels and Benjamins are namesakes of Jewish great-grandpas, the phenomenon can be explained by an interesting theory concerning the cycles that occur in the naming patterns of immigrant families. According to the theory, first-generation immigrants typically renounce any clue to their ethnicity and so choose names for their children prevalent in general society. It is not until the third generation, or even later, that there is enough psychological distance for people to reembrace their ethnic heritage and incorporate it into their lives.

This is evidenced by the naming history of Jewish families in this country. The children of early immigrants turned to the most Anglo-Saxon sounding names they could find, lighting in particular upon aristocratic British surname-names like Stanley and Sheldon, Morton, Milton, and Melvin.

The following chart tracks some representative American Jewish given names from the turn of the century to the present.

ABE	ARTHUR	ALAN	ADAM	ABRAHAM
ANNIE	ANN	ANITA	AMY	ANNIE
BEN	BERNARD	BARRY	BRIAN	BEN
CLARA	CLAIRE	CAROL	CARRIE	CLAIRE
DORA	DOROTHY	DIANE	DEBBIE	DORIAN
FANNY	FRAN	FRANCES	FRANCESCA	FANNY
HARRY	HENRY	HARRIS	HARRISON	HENRY
ISAAC	IRVING	IRA	IAN	ISAAC
JAKE	JEROME	JAMES	JAY	JAKE
JENNY	JEAN	JANICE	JENNIFER	JENNA
LILY	LILIAN	LINDA	LORI	LILY
MAX	MARVIN	MITCHELL	MICHAEL	MAX
MOLLY	MARIAN	MARSHA	MARCY	MOLLY
NELLIE	NORMA	NANCY	NICOLE	NELL
RACHEL	RHODA	ROCHELLE	RICKI	RACHEL
ROSE	RUTH	RENÉE	RANDI	ROSIE
SADIE	SYLVIA	SUSAN	STACY	SADIE
SAM	SHELDON	STEVEN	SCOTT	SAM
SARAH	SELMA	SHEILA	SHELLY	SARAH
SOPHIE	SHIRLEY	SHARON	SHERRY	SOPHIE

Popular belief to the contrary, naming a Jewish child after a deceased relative is not mandated by any religious law or biblical test. Rather, the practice springs from a Jewish folk-lore belief that a person's name is his soul. In the Ashkenazic (Jews whose families originated in middle Europe) tradition, naming a child after a living relative could rob the relative of part of his soul and thus shorten his life. Today, even many nonreligious Jews carry a vestigial resistance toward naming a child after a living relative or friend.

This custom, however, is not practiced by Sephardic Jews (whose origins are in Southern Europe, North Africa, and the Middle East), who will name a child after a living relative. Traditionally, paternal grandparents are honored first, followed by maternal grandparents and then aunts and uncles. Infrequently, the child of a Sephardic family will even be named after a parent.

In both cultures, a baby usually isn't given the exact name of the person he is honoring, but a secular name with the same first letter as that person's Jewish or Hebrew name. The reason is not superstition, but simply that many parents don't like the ancestral name.

Double naming—giving a child both a mainstream and a religious name—began in the Middle Ages when the use of names taken from local languages had become so rampant that rabbis decreed that each Jewish boy be given a Hebrew (or otherwise sanctified) name at the time of his circumcision. Having two names soon became the custom for all Jewish babies; a child would have a sacred name, by which he would be called up to read to Torah, as well as a secular name for nonreligious purposes. First-generation American Jews would take their Hebrew names, say Avraham, and anglicize them to any English name beginning with the same initial, from the obvious Abraham to the more assimilated-sounding Arthur or Arnold.

The revival of the Hebrew language in Israel has prompted many American Jewish families to adopt traditional Hebrew names for their babies. Among the most popular are:

HEBREW NAMES

G I R L S

ADIRA	LIORA/LEORA
ALIZA(H)	MICAELA
ARIEL(LE)	MICHAL
ASHIRA	MORIA(H)
AVIGAIL	OFRA
AVIVA(H)	ORA(H)
AZIZA	PUA(H)
CHAVA	SARAI
DALYA/DALIA	SHIRA(H)
DENORA	TALIA
DINAH	TAMAR
ELAMA	TOVA(H)
GALIA	TZURI(Y)A
GAVRILLA	VARDINA
JOELLA	YAEL
KELILA	YAF(F)A
KIRYA	YONA(H)

B O Y S

ADIN	GILAD
AHARON	ISAIAH
AITAN	JAEL
AMON/AMNON	JONAH
ARI	LAEL
ASA	LEVI
AVI	MALACHI
AVNER	MATAN
AVRAM	NOAM
AZRIEL	ORI
BOAZ	RAM
CHAIM	SHAUL
DOV	TAL
EITAN/EYTAN	URI
ELAD	URIAH
ELI	YAAKOV
ELISHA	YITZHAR
EMANUEL	YOAV
EPHRAIM	YOEL
ERAN	ZACHARIAH
GAVRIEL	ZIV
GIDEON	ZOHAR

THE GOOD BOOK OF NAMES

The Bible, particularly the Old Testament, has always been a prime source of names for children in America, dating back to the Hephzibahs and Zedekiahs of Colonial times. But, even with this timeless source, there are trends and fashions. In our day, Sarah, Benjamin, Jonathan and Joshua, Rachel and Rebecca, Adam and Aaron, popular for the past twenty years, have just about peaked, while Hannah and Leah are rapidly advancing.

Some fresher-sounding choices might include:

F E M A L E

ABIGAIL	BETHIA
ADAH	DEBORAH/
ADINA	DEVORAH
AIAH	DEENA
BATSHEVA/	DELILAH
BATHSHEBA	DINAH

ELISHEVA	MIRIAM
ESTHER	NAOMI
EVE	ORPAH
HADASSAH	SHIFRA
JAEL	TAMAR
JEMIMA/YEMIMA	THIRZA
KETURAH	YEDIDA
KEZIA(H)	ZILLAH
LILITH	ZIPPORAH
MARA	ZORAH (place name)
MICHAL	

MALE

ABEL	ESAU
ABIEL	EZEKIEL
ABNER	EZRA
ABRAHAM	GABRIEL
ABSALOM	GERSHOM, GERSON
ADLAI	GIDEON
AMOS/AMOZ	HIRAM
ASA	ISAAC
ASHER	ISIAH
BOAZ	JABEZ
CALEB	JARED
ELEAZAR	JAVAN
ELI	JEDEDIAH
ELIJAH	JEREMIAH
ELISHA	JETHRO
EMANUEL	JOAB
ENOCH	JOEL/YOEL
EPHRAIM	JONAH

JOSIAH	PHINEAS
JUDAH	RAPHAEL
KENAN	REUBEN
LABAN	SAMSON
LEVI	SAUL
MALACHI	SETH
MICAH	SIMEON
MOSES	SIMON
NATHAN	SOLOMON
NATHANIEL	TOBIAS
NOAH	URIAH/URI
OBADIAH	YOAV
OMAR	ZACHARIAH
OZNI	ZEBADIAH

Fabian, patron saint Of rock and roll, And other unusual, Lively, and surprising Saints' names

If, because of tradition or religion, you want to give your child a saint's name, you don't have to settle for obvious choices like Anne, Cecelia, Anthony, or Joseph. Yes, there really is a Saint Fabian, as well as Saints Chad, Benno, Phoebe, Susanna, and Colette. What follows is a selective list of unexpected saints' names.

F E M A L E

ADELA	AQUILINA
ADELAIDE	ARIADNE
AGATHA	AUDREY
ALBINA	AURIA
ANASTASIA	AVA
ANGELA	BEATRICE
ANGELINA	BEATRIX
ANTONIA	BIBIANA
APOLLONIA	BRIDGET/BRIGID

CANDIDA
CHARITY
CHRISTINA
CLARE
CLAUDIA
CLEOPATRA
CLOTILDA
COLETTE
COLUMBA
CRISPINA
DARIA
DELPHINA
DIANA
DOROTHY
EBBA
EDITH
EMILY
EMMA
EUGENIA
EULALIA
EVA
FABIOLA
FAITH
FELICITY
FLORA
FRANCA
GEMMA
GENEVIEVE
HEDDA
HYACINTH
IDA
ISABEL

JANE
JOANNA
JOAQUINA
JULIA
JULIANA
JUSTINA
LELIA
LEWINA
LOUISA
LUCRETIA
LUCY
LYDIA
MADELEINE
MARCELLA
MARINA
MARTINA
MATILDA
MAURA
MELANIA
MICHELINA
NATALIA
ODILIA
OLIVE
PAULA
PETRONILLA
PHOEBE
PRISCILLA
REGINA
RITA
ROSALIA
SABINA
SALOME

SANCHIA	THEODORA
SERAPHINA	THEODOSIA
SILVA	VERENA
SUSANNA	WINIFRED
TATIANA	ZENOBIA
THEA	ZITA

M A L E

AARON	BERTRAND
ABEL	BLANE
ABRAHAM	BORIS
ADAM	BRENDAN
ADOLF	BRICE
ADRIAN	BRUNO
AIDAN	CHAD
ALBERT	CLEMENT
ALEXANDER	CLETUS
ALEXIS	COLMAN
AMBROSE	CONAN
AMIAS	CONRAD
ANSELM	CORNELIUS
ARNOLD	CRISPIN
ARTEMAS	CYPRIAN
AUBREY	CYRIL
BARDO	DAMIAN
BARNABAS	DANIEL
BARTHOLOMEW	DECLAN
BASIL	DIEGO
BENEDICT	DONALD
BENJAMIN	DUNSTAN
BENNO	EDMUND

EDWIN
ELIAS
EPHRAEM
ERASMUS
ERIC
ERNEST
EUGENE
EUSTACE
FABIAN
FELIX
FERDINAND
FERGUS
FLAVIAN
FLORIAN
GERARD
GILBERT
GILES
GODFREY
GREGORY
GUNTHER
GUY
HERBERT
HILARY
HUBERT
HUGH
HUMBERT
ISAAC
ISIDORE
ISRAEL
JASON
JONAH
JORDAN
JULIAN
JULIUS
JUSTIN
KEVIN
KIERAN
KILIAN
LAMBERT
LEANDER
LEO
LEONARD
LINUS
LLOYD
LUCIAN
LUCIUS
MALACHY
MARIUS
MAXIMILIAN
MEL
MILO
MOSES
NOEL
NORBERT
OLIVER
OSWALD
OTTO
OWEN
PIRAN
QUENTIN
RALPH
RAYMOND
REMI
ROCCO (Italian

version of
Saint Roch)
RODERIC
RUFUS
RUPERT
SAMSON
SEBASTIAN
SILAS
SIMEON
SIMON

SYLVESTER
THEODORE
TITUS
VIRGIL
WILFRED
WOLFGANG
YVES
ZACHARY
ZENO

Parents should choose suitable names for their children, avoiding such as are obscene, ridiculous or impious. It is advisable that the name of a saint or of some other person distinguished for holiness be chosen, for this will be of a spiritual advantage to the child and an edification to others.

—*Codex Iuris Cononici*, Rome, 1917

"It's Mel," Gibson explains, "not Melvin. Mel is actually an old Irish name. They've got a cathedral in Ireland called St. Mel's. I don't really know how Mel got to be a saint. There

was probably some nepotism involved, because
Mel was a cousin of Saint Patrick."

—Mel Gibson, quoted in *Premiere* magazine

ITALIAN BATTALION

Traditional Italian-American families adhere to a strict naming procedure brought over from Italy, in which everybody is named after somebody else. Here's how it works:

First son is named after father's father
First daughter.............. father's mother
Second son .... mother's father
Second daughter.......... mother's mother
Subsequent sons.......... father's brothers, in order of age.
  If you run out, mother's
  brothers.
Subsequent daughters .. father's sisters, in order of age.
  When you finish with them,
  mother's sisters.

This practice radically simplifies the naming decision, especially since, until this generation, most Italian families were so large it was tough to exhaust the entire store of possibilities. It also leads to lots of children with the same names. To prevent too much overlap, variations are permissible and often used, especially for girls' names. Grandma Rosemarie, for instance, may have namesakes called Rose, Maria, Annemarie, Rosanne, and Mary. Grandpa Anthony, whose name cannot be varied as easily, is likely to spawn a veritable legion of Anthonys.

Assimilation, intermarriage, and the trend to smaller families are combining to endanger this sort of name inbreeding. While it's sad to lose such a finely tuned tradition, there is an up side: When you call your child at a family reunion, fifty people don't come running.

ROOTS

Shortly after he took the heavyweight championship from Sonny Liston in 1964, Cassius Clay announced to the world that he had joined the Nation of Islam and was discarding his "slave name" in favor of Cassius X, soon switched to Muhammad Ali. By renaming himself, Ali was in the vanguard of a movement that was to burgeon in the late sixties, when many blacks adopted the Muslim religion and took on—for themselves and for their children—Islamic names. In 1971, basketball star Lew Alcindor—not a Black Muslim but a member of the orthodox Hanafei sect—changed his name to Kareem Abdul-Jabbar. Other black athletes, entertainers, and public figures followed suit.

At the same time, some people were looking back to their African heritage in search of an ethnically valid name, a trend heavily reinforced by the widely seen television miniseries, *Roots*, in 1977. Playwright LeRoi Jones became Imamu Amiri Baraka and soon it was not uncommon to hear tribal names like Ashanti and Akuba in the playground. Still other parents chose to honor heroes of black American history. Playwright and actor Douglas Turner Ward, for instance, abandoned his given birth name of Roosevelt in favor of a combination of the names of abolitionist Frederick Douglass and revolutionary slave Nat Turner.

Black parents who wish to pay homage to their past have a vast menu of unusual names from which to choose. Following is a selection of both Arabic and African names.

ARABIC NAMES

Muslim names usually derive from those of the Prophet Muhammad's descendants or immediate family. There are five hundred variations of the name Muhammad itself; taken together they become the most common boy's name in the world. Other popular Arabic names, such as Karim and Kamil, represent the ninety-nine qualities of God listed in the Koran.

G I R L S

AKILAH	KARIDA
AMINA	LEILA
AYASHA	NIMA
BARAKAH	NUMA
FATIMAH	OMA
HABIBAH	RIDA
HATIMA	RIHANA
HINDA	SELIMA
JAMILA	SHAHAR
JINAN	YASMEEN

B O Y S

ABDEL/ABDUL/
  ABDULLAH
AHMED/AHMAD
ALI
ALLAH
AZIM
DAWUD
FARIO
HAKEEM
HAMID
HANIF
HASHIM
HASSAN
HUSAIN

IBRAHIM
JAFAR
JAMIL
JUMAH
KAMALI
KAMIL
KARIM
KASIM
MALIK
MUHAMMAD and its
  variations
OMAR
RAHMAN

If you have a hundred sons, name them all Muhammad.

—Muslim proverb

AFRICAN NAMES

G I R L S

ABA	JINA
ABINA/ABENA	KANIKA
ADESINA	KATURA
ADIA	KAYA
AKUBA	KIAH
AMMA	LAYLA
APRILI	NEEMA
ASIZA/AZIZA	OBA
BARIKA	RASHIDA
CAMISHA	SHANI
CHIRIGA	TABIA
DALILA	TARANA
FAYOLA	TISA
HASINA	YABA
IMENA	ZAHARA
JANI	

B O Y S

ABASI	BEM
ADOM	KAYIN
AGU	KITO
AJANI	KOSEY/KOSSE
ASHANTI	KWAMIN
ASHON	KWASI
AYANA	LADO
AZIZI	MASUD
BELLO	ODION

OKO   SUDI
RUDO   TANO

He walked there now . . . thinking of names.
Surely, he thought, he and his sister had some
ancestor, some lithe young man with onyx skin
and legs as straight as cane stalks, who had a
name that was real. A name given to him at
birth with love and seriousness. A name that was
not a joke, nor a disguise, nor a brand name.
But who this lithe young man was . . . could
never be known. No. Nor his name.

—Toni Morrison, *Song of Solomon*

Wednesday Is Full of Woe

The Ashantis in West Africa name their children
according to the day of the week on which they
are born. Each day is believed to signify a certain temperament—for example, Monday boys
are quiet and obedient, Wednesday boys fiery
and aggressive. And sure enough, more offen-
ses are committed by Wednesdays than by any
others, with very few delinquents born on (and
so named) Monday.

Names from across The ocean

Let's say you're Irish, and you want to give your child a name that reflects your heritage, but want to find some middle ground between the hackneyed Erin or Sean and too-foreign choices such as Gormghlaith or Maolruadhan. That's what we offer here: mid-range names such as the Irish Keara and Liam—as well as choices from other European locales—that have a distinctly ethnic flavor, yet are pleasing to American tastes.

ENGLISH NAMES

GIRLS

ARAMINTA
FELICITY
GEMMA

JESSAMINE
KERENSA
LIVIA

PHILIPPA
SIDONIE

TABITHA
TAMSIN

B O Y S

ALISTAIR
CLIVE
COLIN
CRISPIN
FLETCHER

INIGO
NIGEL
NOEL
ROBIN
TREVOR

FRENCH NAMES

G I R L S

ANAÏS
ARIANE
CAMILLE
CÉCILE
EUGÉNIE

FRANÇOISE
LUCIENNE
MARINE
NICOLETTE
SYLVIE

B O Y S

ALAIN
ANDRÉ
CLÉMENT
DIDIER
ÉTIENNE

JULIEN
LUC
MAXIME
RAOUL
THIERRY

GERMAN NAMES

G I R L S

AMALIE	KATHARINA
ANNALISE	KATJA
CAROLA	MONIKA
CHRISTIANE	PETRA
ELKE	SENTA

B O Y S

ARNO	LEOPOLD
GÜNTER	MARKUS
JOHANN	MATHIAS
KASPAR	STEFAN
KONRAD	TOBIAS

GREEK NAMES

G I R L S

ATHENA	KALLIOPE
CLIO	OLYMPIA
COSIMA	PALLAS
ELENI	STEFANIA
EVANGELINE	THEODORA

B O Y S

BASIL	DAMIAN
CHRISTOS	HARALAMBOS
CLAUDIOS	NIKOLOS
CONSTANTINE	SEBASTIAN
COSMO	STAVROS

HUNGARIAN/SLAVIC NAMES

G I R L S

ANEZKA	KATERINA
AURELIA	LILIKE
DANICA	MARIKA
FANIA	TEREZA
ILONA	TESIA

B O Y S

DORJAN	KARSTEN
ERNO	KITO
JANOS	ODON
JENO	PIOTR
KAROLY	VILMOS

IRISH NAMES

G I R L S

BRENNA	MAEVE
CAITRIN	MAIREAD
FIONA	MOIRA
KEARA	SINEAD
KEELIN	SIOBHAN

B O Y S

CARRICK	LIAM
DECLAN	MALACHY
DERRY	NEVIN
EAMON	NIALL
KEIRAN	ROHAN

ITALIAN NAMES

G I R L S

ADRIANA	LUCIA
ALLEGRA	ORIANA
CARLOTTA	RENATA
CHIARA	SILVANA
LIA	VITTORIA

B O Y S

ADRIANO
GIORGIO
GREGORIO
LORENZO
LUCIO

MARIO
PAOLO
ROBERTO
TADDEO
VITTORIO

POLISH NAMES

G I R L S

ALINA
CELINA
FELCIA
JANINA
KAMILLA

KASSIA
LILIANNA
RASIA
STASHA
ZOFIA

B O Y S

ANZELM
BORYS
CASIMIR
JANOS
JAREK

MARIUS
MATEUSZ
TOMASZ
ZAREK

RUSSIAN NAMES

G I R L S

ANASTASSIA	KATYA
ANTONINA	KIRA
EVELINA	LARISA
GALINA	NATALYA
IRINA	TATYANA

B O Y S

ALEXANDR	GRIGORI
ALEXEI	IVAN
ANDREI	MIKHAIL
DAVEED	NICOLAI
DIMITRI	ROMAN

SCANDINAVIAN NAMES

G I R L S

ANNIKA	LIV
ASTRID	MARIT
GRETA/E	SONJA
HANNE	TORIL
INGRID	VIVEKA

B O Y S

ANDERS	KRISTIAN
AUDUN	LARS
BJÖRN	MORTEN
FINN	STIAN
HANS	TOR

SCOTTISH NAMES

G I R L S

AILEEN	ISOBEL
BETHIA	LILIAS
CATRIONA	LORNA
ELSPETH	MOIRA
GILLIAN	ROBENA

B O Y S

ANGUS	GAVIN
CALUM	GRAHAM
CAMERON	LACHLAN
DOUGALD	MUNGO
DUNCAN	TAVIS

SPANISH NAMES

G I R L S

BLANCA	LUISA
CARMELA	MARISOL
CONSUELO	PILAR
ELENA	SARITA
ESTRELLA	SERAFINA

B O Y S

ALEJANDRO	LUIS
ANTONIO	MANUEL
ENRIQUE	ORLANDO
ENZO	RAFAEL
FEDERICO	RAUL

WELSH NAMES

G I R L S

BRONWYN	MEREDITH
BRYN	MORGAN
ELEN/ELIN	RHIANNON
GWYNETH	RHONWYN
MAIR	WINIFRED

B O Y S

BEVAN	GRIFFITH
CAI	LLEWELYN
DYLAN	OWEN
EVAN	RHYS
GARETH	WYNNE

When I was a kid, I didn't know anybody named Heather or Joshua. In my neighborhood, boys had solid workmanlike names: Stanley, Chester, Walter, Norbert, Albert, Henry, or Joe. Girls had in-the-kitchen names like Bertha, Dorothy, Helen, Mildred, Eleanor, Mary, Lucille, and Gertrude.

But today, it's not unusual to find people with monikers like Heather Potkowski, Kevin Bongiorino, Danielle Goldberg. No wonder young people grow up confused about who they are.

—Mike Royko, *Chicago Tribune* syndicated column

INTO THE POOL

Some foreign-born celebs—most of them in the movies—have added their names to our national reservoir. Several of their names have gained widespread popularity, while others have seen only occasional use. The Names who have inspired these names include:

F E M A L E

ANOUK Aimée
BRIGITTE Bardot
BRITT Ekland
CLAUDETTE Colbert
DANIELLE Darrieux
DENISE Darcel
ELKE Sommer
GINA Lollobrigida
GLYNIS Johns
GREER Garson
GRETA Garbo
HAYLEY Mills
HEDY Lamarr
ILONA Massey
INGER Stevens
INGRID Bergman
LILIA Skalia
LIV Ullmann
MARLENE Dietrich

MARTINA Navratilova
MELINA Mercouri
MICHÈLE Morgan
MOIRA Shearer
NADIA Comaneci
NASTASSIA Kinski
PALOMA Picasso
PETULA Clark
POLA Negri
RUTGER Hauer
SAMANTHA Eggar
SHEENA Easton
SIGNE Hasso
SIMONE Signoret
SINEAD O'Connor
SIOBHAN McKenna
SONJA Henie
SOPHIA Loren
VIVECA Lindfors

MALE

ALAIN Delon
ALISTAIR Cooke
BASIL Rathbone
BJÖRN Borg
CLIVE Brook
DIRK Bogarde
DYLAN Thomas
ELIA Kazan
EMLYN Williams
ERROL Flynn
MARCELLO
   Mastroianni

MIKHAIL Baryshnikov
NICOL Williamson
NOËL Coward
OMAR Sharif
PABLO Picasso
RAUL Julia
REX Harrison
SEAN Connery
TREVOR Howard
YVES Montand
ZUBIN Mehta

FAMILY TIES

YOU SAY MARIA, I SAY MARYA; LET'S CALL THE WHOLE THING OFF

One of the few advantages of single parenthood must surely be that you get to choose your child's name all by yourself. When you become enchanted with Flora, there's no one around who will say, "Sounds like someone who sells violets in an alley." When you decide absolutely on Kevin, nobody pretends to gag, saying, "Forget it. I went to school with a Kevin who had bad breath." You don't have to deal with anyone wanting to name your child Rudolph after his great-grandfather or Sabra after the heroine of her favorite novel.

However, most people go into parenthood in pairs, and most couples choose their baby's name together. While having a child may, more than any other event, make you and your mate feel as one, choosing the child's name can highlight how separate you really are. Each of you brings your own associations, family history, ethnic background, taste, and imagination to the naming of a child. Attempting to merge all those elements and arrive at a name you both love can sometimes seem as futile as trying to predict your child's genetic makeup.

Some couples avoid wrangling over names by agreeing beforehand that one partner—usually the wife—will choose the children's names. Other husbands and wives split the selection process: He chooses the boys' names and she selects the girls', for instance, or she picks a name for the first child and he decides on the second. This sort of division of mental labor is usually found in couples who divide other kinds of decisions: He decides how to spend the money and she decides which laundry detergent to use, for example. In other words, it's old-fashioned.

Modern dads quite rightly expect an equal voice in choosing the name of the baby whose bottom they're going to diaper half the time, as do modern moms, who will be footing half the baby-sitter's salary. In addition, the fact that couples are marrying—and having children—later in life complicates the naming decision: The longer the separate "past" each partner has, the more potential for disagreement about names. In this case, names with happy old associations can be even more of a no-no than those with unpleasant ones. Resist the urge to commemorate that wonderful weekend you had in Capri five years ago with Carlo or Carlotta.

Some couples attempt to get a jump on the naming-decision process by beginning discussions long before they have a nine-month deadline, even before they have cemented their status as a couple. Names for potential children can become a symbolic turning point in a courtship. "My boyfriend says we can't even talk about getting married until

I agree to name our first son Bill," one woman told us. To him, Bill is the epitome of a good, solid name, like "My Boy Bill" in *Carousel*; to her, it's the retarded title character in the Mickey Rooney film. Wedding plans are still on hold.

Another couple, married for three months, takes long drives in the country to discuss names for their hypothetical child. "My husband likes the name Harry," says the woman. "Everybody in my family thinks it sounds really awful, like a janitor or something."

And a couple who argued about their son's name throughout the pregnancy were shocked in the delivery room by the arrival of a daughter. The husband's first words upon her birth: "Well, I guess that settles the Henry question." While it may have rendered moot their months-long argument over whether the name Henry sounded wimpy or strong, it introduced another question: what to name a girl.

Is there a way to sidestep all this angst in your search for a mutually satisfying name? Part of the solution lies in understanding the problem.

First, you should realize that issues such as differing associations to the names of family members, childhood friends and classmates, and past loves can never truly be resolved: If you went to school with a wonderful Tracy and your mate knew a terrible one, neither of you will ever be able to shake the association.

Differences in taste are stickier. You'll find that if you and your spouse tend to agree on style in clothes, furniture, music, and movies, you'll have an easier time agreeing on a name, or at least coming up with a group of names from which to choose. If, on the other hand, you're one of those couples who battle to the death over whether to buy an antique or a high-tech couch, you may be facing the same kind of fashion issue over choosing a name.

It helps to be aware that picking a name can uncover deep-seated issues of masculinity and femininity. A man may push for macho boys' names and ultrafeminine girls' names; a woman may push for ambisexual names for either. Obviously, what's at stake here is more than a name; it encompasses how you envision your son or daughter, and how you view the sexes in general.

How you see yourself vis à vis your own name can also breed disagreement between you and your mate. Growing up as a Ruth, say, may make you want to give your child a bouncy, fashionable name, while your husband, Jody, may wish to counter his own experience by choosing a name that's classic and grown-up.

While understanding all these problems may not make them go away, it can spark more enlightened naming discussions. Here are some concrete things you can do to arrive at a name that's an optimum choice for both of you:

Talk about issues like image and sexuality before you talk about names: What do you each hope for in a child? Is your fantasy child energetic or studious, "all-boy" or gentle, feminine or tomboy? Coming to agreement on these matters, or at least getting them out in the open, can help when you're choosing a name—not to mention raising your child.

Rule out all names of ex-girlfriends and ex-boyfriends. No matter how much you like the name Jill, do not proceed with it if your husband had a long, torrid affair with a Jill way back when. Do not tell yourself you'll forget: You won't, and neither will he.

Make a "no" list as well as a "yes" list: Most couples only make lists of the names they like; it can help to make lists, too, of the names that are absolutely out for each of you. Include those you'd rule out for personal reasons (the name of the guy who dumped you in high school and the roommate who stole all your clothes) as well as names you simply hate. Agree that neither of you will bring up the names on each other's "absolutely not" lists, no matter how much you like them or how neutral they may be for you.

Avoid using the name selection process as an opportunity to criticize each other's loved ones: When he campaigns for naming your son Morton after his father, this is not an excuse to tell him how much you hate his father, no matter how much you hate the name Morton. Surely you can find enough negative things to say about the name itself without widening the battlefield.

Investigate the reasons for each other's choices: Let's say you love a name your spouse hates. Instead of fighting over the name itself, explore what it is about the name that appeals to you. Figuring out whether you like a name because it's classic, or feminine, or stylish, say, can lead you to other names with the same characteristics that you both may like.

Remember that parenthood is a joint venture: Just as your child will be a unique blend of characteristics from both of you, so should you endeavor to arrive at a name that combines each of your sensibilities and tastes. It will take some enlightened thinking, searching, and negotiating, but that's what this book is all about.

PUTTING THE NAME BEFORE THE BABY

In this age of amniocentesis and ultrasound, many parents have the option of knowing their baby's sex—and thus making a firm decision on a name—long before his or her arrival.

While these medical advances have been a boon for mothers and babies alike, and knowing your child's sex can cut the work of choosing a name in half, we nevertheless caution against telling the world your child's gender and name months before his or her actual arrival.

Announcing in mid-pregnancy that a boy named Dawson is waiting to be born can have a dampening effect on his entrance into the world. For one thing, other people tend to draw a more or less complete picture of little Dawson's looks and personality, based on his name and their knowledge of his parents, long before they get a chance to meet him! For another, you may find that other people are actually less eager to meet him. Instead of waiting by the phone for news of your baby's sex and name, they may receive your announcement with a bored, "Oh, Dawson's finally here."

The only real advantage we can cite for sharing your child's name before his birth is not really that much of a plus: People can give you shower gifts of little T-shirts with Dawson spelled out on the back.

MAUDE: No beautiful names, okay? Not Nicholas or Christopher or Adam or Jonathan.
ROB: Or Jennifer or Gwyneth or Cherish or Innocence.
MAUDE: And no politics, right? Not America or . . . Peace

and Freedom . . . just short and to the point . . . Joe, Gus, Eddie. Not Edward, Eddie.

ROB: Sue, Pat—American Bandstand names, right? So it's settled. If it's a girl, it's Tallulah No-Nukes Salinger.

MAUDE: And if it's a boy, it's Bartholomew Zachary Save-the-Whales Chastity-Belt Salinger.

—*Micki and Maude*, 1984

In Search of a Girl's Name

. . . Jane stroked the pale brown down on the baby's head. "What does she look like to you? She looks like a Miranda to me."

"No."

"No."

"Samantha? Christiana?"

"No exotic names."

"Those aren't exotic. How about Gwendolyn?"

"How about Mary?"

"Are you serious, Nick? . . . Mary Cobleigh. It sounds like a barmaid. But Maria might not be bad . . ."

"Too Catholic. . . ."

"How about Tuttle? . . ."

"I hate that," Nicholas said. "I keep meeting all these girls named Heywood and Lockhart

and they always had dumb-bunny nicknames.
Although . . . I sort of like Heissenhuber Cobleigh. It has a distinguished ring to it. A fine old
name. A noble—"

"If you don't stop I'll put Tammy on the birth
certificate."

"I've got it, Jane!"

"This should be terrific."

"Dorothy."

"Even John would be better than that. . . ."

"Come on, now. We need a nice, plain,
pretty name. Caroline."

"It sounds like we're copying the Kennedys."

"All right. Ann."

". . . A little too simple. Even with an e."

"Elizabeth."

"I like that," Jane said. "But . . . she doesn't
look like an Elizabeth."

"If you name her Zelda than she'll look like
a Zelda."

"No, she won't. . . . Let me think. Olivia and
Abigail are out. And Winifred. . . . I know,"
Jane said. "Victoria."

"Victoria?"

"Victoria Cobleigh. It's a little regal,
but that's okay. . . . What do you
think?"

"You're not going to call her Tory, are
you?"

"No! Maybe Vicky, if she's athletic and en-

ergetic like you. But otherwise just beautiful, elegant, gorgeous, adorable, sweet, cuddly—"
"Victoria."

—Susan Isaacs, *Almost Paradise*

BABY, JR.

The easiest solution to the question of what to name a baby boy is to simply repeat the father's name, appending to it the letters Jr. Although this practice is fading out of fashion, it does have certain advantages: a direct link with a progenitor, the pride that goes with carrying on a family name.

But the disadvantages can outweigh the benefits. The child may well feel he's inheriting an identity along with a name, that he's merely a paler shadow of his father, that he will always be number two.

If a boy is actually addressed by the same name as his father, countless confusions will arise, from the most obvious, such as "Which Donald do you want, Big Donald or Little Donald?" on the phone, and fathers and sons opening (and reading) each other's mail, to more subtle ones, like mother having to call the two most important males in her life, husband and son, by the same name.

On the other hand, if the child is called Junior, he is somewhat dehumanized, almost like being referred to as a number, and a lesser number than his father at that. More common is for the child to be known by a familiar, childish form of the name, a practice that spawns its own perils. Dad is Don and junior is Donny, forever locked by his name into an adolescent (or younger) image of himself that persists long after he leaves home. Or, even worse, he might be known to the world as Bud, Buster, Butch, Sonny, Skip, or Chip.

Giving a boy the same name as his father and grandfather—making him a III—is a somewhat different issue. On the positive side, it could be argued that you're carrying on a family tradition rather than purely indulging in egotism. And honorable WASP nicknames for IIIs—Tripp, Tre, or Trey—are not quite as humiliating as the ones many juniors are saddled with. On the down side, little Frederick or Albert the third has the image of not one but two grown-up men to live up to, with a fairly strong (and potentially overwhelming) mandate to carry on the family tradition.

Only one president in the history of the United States has been a junior—James Earl Carter, Jr., who, as we all know, insisted on being known by his childhood nickname of Jimmy. Gerald Ford was born Leslie Lynch King, Jr., but his name was changed when he was adopted by his stepfather. Relatively few juniors are to be found among high achievers in sports or the fine arts. However, there are lots of military men, junior grade.

How to avoid the pitfalls of juniordom and still name your son after his father? You could go the royal route and name him Donald Dalton Duckworth II. Or the child could be given a different middle name, say Donald Duncan Duckworth, be called Duncan by the family, and later sign his memos D. Duncan Duckworth. But before taking this approach, remember the old saying, "Don't trust anyone who parts his name on the side."

Some juniors who made names for themselves

KAREEM ABDUL-JABBAR (Ferdinand Lewis Alcindor, Jr.)
EDWARD ALBERT, Jr.
MUHAMMAD ALI (Cassius Marcellus Clay, Jr.)
JOSEPH W. ALSOP, Jr.
ARTHUR ASHE, Jr.
ED BEGLEY, Jr.
HARRY BELAFONTE (Harold George Belafonte, Jr.)
MARLON BRANDO, Jr.
YUL BRYNNER (Taidje Khan, Jr.)
WILLIAM F. BUCKLEY, Jr.
JAMES CAGNEY (James Francis Cagney, Jr.)
JIMMY CARTER (James Earl Carter, Jr.)
LON CHANEY, Jr.
CHARLIE CHAPLIN (Charles Spencer Chaplin, Jr.)
CHUBBY CHECKER (Ernest Evans, Jr.)
VAN CLIBURN (Harvey Lavan Cliburn, Jr.)
JIMMY CONNORS (James Scott Connors, Jr.)
JACKIE COOPER (John Cooper, Jr.)
BILL COSBY (William H. Cosby, Jr.)
HUME CRONYN (Hume Blake, Jr.)
SAMMY DAVIS, Jr.
ROBERT DE NIRO, Jr.
JOHN DENVER (Henry John Deutschendorf, Jr.)
TROY DONAHUE (Merle Johnson, Jr.)
MIKE DOUGLAS (Michael Delaney Dowd, Jr.)
ROBERT DONNEY, Jr.
CLINTON EASTWOOD, Jr.
BUDDY EBSEN (Christian Ebsen, Jr.)

DOUGLAS FAIRBANKS, Jr.(Douglas Elton Thomas Ullman, Jr.)

ALBERT FINNEY, Jr.

LOUIS GOSSETT, Jr.

ALEXANDER M. HAIG, Jr.

WILLIAM RANDOLPH HEARST, Jr.

VAN HEFLIN (Emmett Evan Heflin, Jr.)

HAL HOLBROOK (Harold Rowe Holbrook, Jr.)

WILLIAM HOLDEN (William Franklin Beedle, Jr.)

OLIVER WENDELL HOLMES, Jr.

ROCK HUDSON (Roy Harold Scherer, Jr.)

HENRY JAMES, Jr.

STACY KEACH (Walter Stacy Keach, Jr.)

BUSTER KEATON (Joseph Francis Keaton, Jr.)

MARTIN LUTHER KING, Jr.

ALAN LADD, Jr.

ALFRED LUNT, Jr.

TIP O'NEILL (Thomas P. O'Neill, Jr.)

FESS PARKER, Jr.

TYRONE POWER, Jr.

ROBERT REDFORD (Charles Robert Redford, Jr.)

BURT REYNOLDS (Burton Leon Reynolds, Jr.)

JASON ROBARDS, Jr.

MICKEY ROONEY (Joe Yule, Jr.)

ARTHUR SCHLESINGER, Jr.

RIP TORN (Elmore Torn, Jr.)

KURT VONNEGUT, Jr.

ROBERT WAGNER, Jr.

HANK WILLIAMS, Jr.

WILLIAM WRIGLEY, Jr.

FRANK ZAPPA (Francis Vincent Zappa, Jr.)

EFREM ZIMBALIST, Jr.

TOM CRUISE (Thomas Cruise Mapother IV)
OSCAR HAMMERSTEIN II
OREL LEONARD HERSCHEISER, IV
LEE MAJORS (Harvey Lee Yeary II)
JACK LEMMON (John Uhler Lemmon III)
EDWIN MEESE III
CLIFF ROBERTSON (Clifford Parker Robertson III)
TOM SMOTHERS (Thomas Bolyn Smothers III)
ADLAI STEVENSON III
LOUDON WAINWRIGHT III

Junior spacemen

Although it isn't a written requirement, being a junior certainly seems to help one's chances of getting into the space program. Juniors who have been launched include:

EDWIN E. ALDRIN, Jr.
CHARLES BASSETT II
GUION S. BLUFORD, Jr.
CHARLES F. BOLDEN, Jr.
ROY D. BRIDGES, Jr.
CHARLES CONRAD, Jr.
L. GORDON COOPER, Jr.
CHARLES M. DUKE, Jr.
JOHN H. GLENN, Jr.
RICHARD F. GORDON, Jr.
FRED W. HAISE, Jr.
HENRY W. HARTSFIELD, Jr.
ROBERT H. LAWRENCE, Jr.
JAMES A. LOVELL, Jr.

JAMES A. LOVELL, Jr.
THOMAS K. MATTINGLY II
ELLIOT SEE, Jr.
WALTER M. SCHIRRA, Jr.
BREWSTER H. SHAW, Jr.
ALAN B. SHEPARD, Jr.
JOHN L. SWIGART, Jr.
EDWARD H. WHITE II

. . . . In the world of juniors, I was one of the lucky ones. I was never called "Junior" as a nickname. I knew one Junior for years without ever knowing his real name. He and other Juniors will tell you that Junior is their real name and sign it that way on a greeting card or a letter. These are the guys people probably have in mind when they ask me if I have a fragile sense of identity because of my juniorhood. . . .
I think that when I was named for my father, the intention was that my name not be simply a utile thing, not be just a handy sound to summon a boy when the garbage needs to be taken down. When a child is named, it is an attempt to define the child. And my definition is my father. I thank my parents for their vote of confidence and I hope I live up to my name. . . .

—Rafael A. Suarez, Jr., "Being a Jr.,"
The New York Times Magazine

SIBLING NAMES
(FOR FIRST-TIME PARENTS ALSO)

If you're having your second, third, fourth child or beyond, you have probably already experienced the inherent difficulties and dilemmas involving sibling names. Ideally, the names you choose for later children should "go with" the name you picked for your first child: They should be harmonious in rhythm and style. At the same time, names of later children should be different enough from the first child's name to avoid confusion. Yes, there are families with a Jane and a Jean, a Larry and a Harry, an Ellen and an Eleanor, but the resulting mix-ups do not seem worth the cuteness.

The real problem with sibling names arises because most parents don't consider later names when they choose the first. But the first choice sets the pattern, narrowing future options. Here's how it works:

Because we have personal experience with this one, let's say you decided to name your first child, a girl, Rory. Good enough, but now you're about to have your second. Names that rhyme are out: Goodbye Laurie, Corey, Glory, Maury, Tory, et al. So too with similar-sounding names: everything in the Rose family, the Mary family, the Doria group, the Lauras, Coras, Noras, and Floras, not to mention Larry, Gerry, Terry; Rowen, Rourke, Rollo. You get the idea.

Also, because Rory is such a distinctively Celtic name, it would sound odd with a name from a different ethnic background. Rory and Francesca won't do, for example. In terms of image, Rory is clearly a High-Energy name. Would it be fair to pair her name with one from the Intellectual Power group? Would a little sister named Ruth, for example, always feel bookwormish by contrast; would Rory, conversely, feel flighty in comparison? Another consideration is the name's ambisexuality. Choosing a sister's name from the Feminine or Feminissima group—Angelica, for instance, or Melissa— might not only sound discordant but could make the two girls feel differently about their sexuality. And if the sibling is a boy, giving him an ambisexual name could make matters even more confusing. A girl named Rory with a brother named Ashley? It just wouldn't work. Finally, Rory is a somewhat unusual name, and a more classic choice for a brother or sister could also strike the wrong chord. Rory and Jane? Rory and John? Somehow, they just don't belong together.

Further complications set in if you have changed your ideas about names after living with your real live first choice for a few years. You may regret choosing an ambisexual name like Rory because of the confusion over whether the child was a boy or a girl, and may also wish you had chosen a more common name that was easier for the child to pronounce and for others to understand. You may really want to name your second child Jane or John, and yet not feel comfortable with those choices.

The point of all this is to encourage you to consider future possibilities when you're choosing the name of your first child. If your two favorite names are Anna and Hannah, for example, realize that picking one now rules out the other forever. When you're deciding among several names, consider the future implications of each. Imagining which names might follow for other children may help you narrow the field.

What, in particular, works and what doesn't? Without taste or value judgments on the specific names, we can tell you some instances of sibling names we're familiar with that do work. Jane and William, for instance, or Sam and Lily. Both pairings are good because, for one, the girls' names are clearly feminine and the boys' clearly masculine. The style is consistent: fashionable, but not to the point of cliché. And the names sound well together but do not sound confusingly alike. Another good brother-and-sister combo is Elizabeth and Charles, called Libby and Charley. Both are classic names that happen to be in style now, and both nicknames are gently old-fashioned, more compatible than, say, Liza and Chuck would be.

Two brothers whose names catch the right rhythm are Felix and Leo. Both are traditional names—saints' names in fact—that, because they hadn't been widely used for some years, have an appealingly offbeat quality. The *x* and the *o* endings provide different but equally unusual sounds for the two names, and they are further related by both being feline.

We know a family of three girls named Melissa, Danielle, and Lauren. Their mother wanted to name the third daughter Patricia. But the classic Patricia—or Pat or Patti—simply did not sound like the sister of the trendier Melissa and Danielle, so Lauren she became.

Fictional children, whose writer "parents" choose all the names at once for kids years apart in age, are often models for name groups that catch the appropriate rhythm: Mallory, Alex, and Jennifer Keaton of television's *Family Ties*, for instance. All euphonic, trendy names, although the mainstream Jennifer stands out a bit, reflecting her TV parents' move toward comformity. When the fictional Keaton mom was pregnant with a fourth child, Jennifer suggested the names Charo and Shecky, but no one took her ideas seriously. The baby was called, predictably, Andrew.

One of the most discordant fictional sets of sibling names

in recent times has been Hannah and her sisters, Holly and Lee, in the Woody Allen film. While the movie was hailed as a triumph for its realism, these three names were anything but believable. The only thing that relates Hannah and Holly is the initial H; beyond that, Hannah is a Biblical name, old world and serious, while Holly is an invented name not used at all until this century and not widely until the 1960s. Holly and Lee, meanwhile, are more consistent in style and tone, but echo each other in sound. Hannah and Lee sound more like sisters than Hannah and Holly do, but even so, Hannah and Leah would have been closer to the mark. In fact, Hannah, Helen, and Leah sound as if they were born of the same parents, while Hannah, Holly, and Lee sound like three women who just happen to be at the same party, which may have been Woody Allen's intention after all.

When the name of a fictional character breaks rank with those of his or her siblings, there's usually some symbolism involved. The classic case is *Little Women*'s Meg, Jo, Beth, and Amy. Even if you haven't read the book, guess which one was the tomboy with ambitions greater than her sisters'.

So too in real life, where the child with a name that is "different" from those of his brothers and sisters may also feel different in spirit. We know of a family with four children named Mary, Christopher, Nicole, and Alexandra. It's clear here too which one considers herself the odd child out.

If you already have your first child and are choosing a name for a sibling, keep the following guidelines in mind:

Don't be cute: No rhymes, sound plays, precious pairings. Resist the temptation, for example to name Daisy's sister Maisie, Darcy, or Hyacinth.

Don't fall into the same initial trap: A trend of the fifties and sixties was to choose sibling names all starting with the same letter. Sometimes, parents didn't consider the consequences if they had chosen to start with the letter E and happened to have, say, five boys. Edward was fine for the first, Eliot okay for the second, but by the birth of their fifth son they were stuck with choices like Earl, Elmer, and Egbert. While few parents have five children today, the same-initial trend should be avoided as dated and overly precious.

Do maintain consistency of style, image, sex, and tradition: This rule is to be interpreted loosely, but, as detailed in the example of Rory, sibling names should ideally stay in the same, well, family.

Be careful about sexual distinctions: If you choose a boyish name for your daughter, and later have a son, go with a boy's name that is clearly masculine. So too if you give your boy an ambisexual name; both he and his little sister will fare better if her name is distinctly feminine. The names of same-sex children should not have widely divergent sexual images: Bruno's brother shouldn't be named Blair, for instance, nor should Belinda's sister.

Avoid using two names with the same nickname: This problem usually crops up when parents, hoping for a junior, despair at the third girl and name her Roberta or Christina or Geraldine. She then becomes Bobbie or Chris or Gerry. When her long-awaited little brother is born five years later, he is named Robert or Christopher or Gerald. Try as the parents might to prevent it, they may end up with a Bobbie and a Bobby, Chris and Chris, or Gerry and Gerry, in addition, of course, to Bobby, Chris, or Gerry Sr. The trend toward smaller families has headed off most occurrences of this problem in recent years, but it still happens. If you're entirely positive that if you ever have a boy you'll name him Christopher, don't name a girl Christina when you give up hope on having a son, or vice versa. Accidents do happen.

GEORGES V

Boxer George Foreman named three of his sons George, one daughter Georgette, and another daughter Frita George.

Along the same lines, University of Oregon sprinter Curtis Ray Wilson, Jr.—son of Curtis Ray Wilson, Sr.—has a younger brother named Curtis Ray Wilson III.

Double Trouble

Twins offer a rare opportunity for parents to choose two related names at the same time, but also multiply the difficulties inherent in sibling names. With twins, it can be more tempting to use rhyme, sound play, and same-initial names, but in our opinion pairings like Eddie and Teddy, Faith and Charity, or Charles and Charlene should be relegated to a time capsule. While same-initial names that are clearly distinct from one another, such as Ross and Rachel, twin children of Jane Pauley and Garry Trudeau, are okay, different-initial names that are consistent in style and tone are preferable.

Some celebrity examples that work: Cybill Shepherd's Ariel and Zack; Meredith Baxter-Birney and David Birney's Mollie and Peter; Ron Howard's Paige and Jocelyn. In all these cases, the names are distinct from each other yet make a harmonious pair—exactly what most parents would want for the twins themselves.

Two examples of twin names that don't work—Debby Boone's Gabrielle and Dustin, and Mia Farrow and André Previn's Matthew and Sascha—fall short for the same reason: Each set has one sexually distinct name and one ambi name. Based on the names alone, one would surmise that they were both boy-girl pairs. In fact, Gabrielle and Dustin are twin girls, and Matthew and Sascha are both boys.

Whatever the sex of the children, twin names should present a compatible image. As detailed in the discussion on sibling names, pairings like Gigi and Walter or Candida and Jennifer are too discordant. Gigi's twin would better be named, perhaps, Barnaby; Walter's sister might be Margaret; Candida's twin could conceivably be called Isabella; and Jennifer's obvious other half is—who else?—Jason.

Ariel and Zack get their birth certificate first names [Molly and Cyrus] from Cybill's great-great-grandparents. Their middle names come right out of a baby book "from A to Z," says Cybill.

—*People* magazine

WHOSE NAME IS IT, ANYWAY?

It is Thanksgiving. You and your sister-in-law, both newly pregnant, are sitting with the rest of the family around the table. Talk turns to names.

"If we have a boy, of course he will be Richard the Third," says your sister-in-law, smiling sweetly at your father. Your brother, Richard Jr., beams.

You, on the other hand, choke on your cranberry sauce. Ever since you were a little girl, you've wanted to name your first son Richard. Besides being your father's name, it's also your husband's father's name, your brother's name, and your favorite boy's name in all the world.

"We were planning on Richard, too," you manage to sputter.

"You can't have it," booms your brother. "Clearly it's our name."

"There's room for two Richards in the family," you reason. "We'll just use different nicknames."

"That's stupid," your brother says. "Ricky and Richie?"

"Now, now," soothes your mother. "What if you have girls?"

"Amanda," you and your brother say in unison.

If you and your spouse have proliferating siblings, the issue of who gets to use which names is one you may have to face. And a difficult issue it is. Does a son have absolute dibs on the father's name? Is there room in a family for two cousins with the same name? Is there a pecking order for who gets traditional family names? Is getting there first a good enough reason to usurp somebody else's name? Can you set claims on a name to begin with?

How you answer these questions depends a lot on your individual family. In some families, the oldest son has eternal right to his father's name, even if he never has a son of his own. In others, it's first come, first served, with the understanding that there will be no later duplications. And some families just play catch-as-catch-can, and worry later about how they'll deal with three cousins named, say, Eric.

If you anticipate some name-wrestling within your own family, keep the following tips in mind:

Announce your choices early on: If you have an absolute favorite name you're sure you will use, don't make a secret of it. Planting it in everyone's mind as "your" name can help avoid problems later.

Don't steal someone else's name: We're not talking about naming your baby Letitia, unaware that, on the same day in a different state, your sister is naming her baby Letitia. We're talking about naming your baby Letitia when your sister has been saying since she was fifteen that her fondest wish in life was to have a little girl named Letitia. And your sister is eight months pregnant. And knows she's having a girl.

Avoid carbon copies: Two little Caroline Townsend Smiths in a close-knit family is one too many. If you want to use the same first and middle names that a sibling uses, can you live with a different nickname—Carrie, for instance? Or can you vary the middle name, so that, at least within the family, one cousin is called Caroline Townsend and the other, say, Caroline Louise? The only case in which two cousins named Caroline Townsend and called Caroline can work is if they have different last names.

Honor family traditions: If the oldest child of the oldest child in your family is always named Taylor, don't break rank, unless your oldest sibling is a nun, priest, or Gay Rights organizer and formally renounces rights to the name.

Take unintentional, unimportant duplications in stride: We know two sisters-in-law, living across the country from each other, who were pregnant at the same time: Jane due in January and Anne in April. During their annual Christmas Eve phone conversation, Jane said she was sure she'd have a boy, and that they were planning to name him Edward. "That's our name," gasped Anne. "Too bad," Jane said blithely. After a few minutes of intense anxiety, Anne decided Jane was right. Neither had officially "claimed" Edward, nor was it a name with any family significance. It would be as ridiculous to insist that Jane change her choice at the eleventh hour as it would be to deny her own son the name just so it wouldn't duplicate that of a cousin he'd see, at best, once a year. Besides, Jane favored the nickname Eddie, while Anne preferred Ted. P.S.: Due to mitigating circumstances, neither baby was named Edward. They ended up Juliet and Josephine.

NAME IN THE MIDDLE

What of your child's middle name?

The strongest trend today is to give your baby a middle name that has meaning. It might be your maiden name, another family surname, the name of someone close to you, or a name with more personal symbolic meaning. Many first-born sons who are not juniors are still given their fathers' names as middle names; increasingly, daughters are getting their mothers' first names as middle names.

Another trend, sparked by the new generation of royal babies, is to give your child more than one middle name, à la little Prince William Arthur Philip Louis, to honor all the relatives in one fell swoop.

You may want to balance an unusual first name with a more solid middle name, or vice versa, if you're unsure of your choice and want to give your child an option later. Or perhaps you feel obligated by tradition or family pressure to give your child a name you absolutely hate: Its place is tucked discreetly in the middle.

Still another increasingly popular option is to give your child no middle name at all. A growing number of parents feel that unless a middle name has some personal meaning, it serves no purpose and may border on the pretentious; others feel that a middle name is "wasted" on a girl, who may drop it when she marries, slotting her maiden name in the middle. (With more and more women keeping their original last names after marriage, this argument no longer stands up.)

What is decidedly out of fashion is giving your child a "throwaway" middle name—a euphonic if insignificant bridge between the first and last name. These are the Anns, Sues, and Lees of our childhoods, names that no one particularly liked or cared about, but that sounded right to the fifties ear following Lisa or Barbara or Karen.

Even more passé (except in the South, where the practice has always been beyond fashion) is giving your child a throwaway middle name you don't throw away—naming her Lisa Ann, for instance, and calling her Lisa Ann.

THE NAME BECOMES THE CHILD

Finally comes the day when you hold your live child in your arms and make a final decision on a real live name. At that point, all the lists you've made, the considerations you've weighed, and the options you've juggled fall by the wayside and you and your child are left with your ultimate choice.

What happens then?

Well, on one hand, the struggle over Miranda vs. Molly seems less crucial in the face of three A.M. feedings, colic, and the high cost of diapers. And it doesn't take very long for your baby's persona to dominate the name, for your baby to become his or her name. For the first two weeks, you may find yourself still calling little Miranda "It"; for the next few, you may feel self-conscious each time you pronounce the name; but a month later you'll find that when you say "Miranda" you don't hear the sound of the name but see instead your child's curved lips and dark curls.

On the other hand, once you've settled on a name, you deal with its myriad implications, often for the first time. You may discover, for instance, that your Aunt Elizabeth is not satisfied to be honored by a mere middle name, that people on the street do not necessarily assume Jordan is a girl, and that friends have to suppress a snicker when you tell them you've named your son Henry.

This may not be fun. This may cause you to retrieve your original lists of possibilities and say to your spouse in the middle of the night, "Maybe we should have named him Michael." And of course, it is possible to change a child's name two days or two months or even two years after you've given it, but it's not easy for many reasons and it's not what we're considering here.

Better than contemplating a name change would be to mull over the fact that choosing one option—in names as in everything else—always means forgoing all others. That the name you've selected inevitably becomes influenced by reality, while the ones you've rejected remain fantasies, entirely pleasant because you alone control them. That in fact if you had chosen Michael, say, you might then be worrying about its ordinariness, might be wishing in the middle of the night that you had gone with something more distinctive like . . . Henry.

Obviously, much of the value of this book is that it helps you anticipate the real world repercussions of a name. And much of the impetus for writing it came from our own experiences and those of our friends in choosing names for children and living with the choices.

One of our friends, for instance, has two children: Emily and Jeremy. "When Emily was born we were living in the country and it seemed like a really special, unusual name," she says. "Then when she was a few months old we moved to the city and I discovered that there were little Emilys everywhere. I felt terrible. I would listen in the playground for other kids named Emily, I would pore over nursery school class lists for other Emilys, and if she was the only Emily I'd feel so relieved. On one hand I feel badly because it seems as if the name is a cliché, but there also aren't so many Emilys as I'd originally feared."

Our friend pinpoints another reason why she was unaware of how widely used the name Emily was (and another reason we wrote this book): "Having a first child I didn't really know any other young parents. I had no idea what people were talking about when they named their kids or what the new style was. My idea of a trendy name was still Barbara or Sue."

What then of Jeremy's name? "That one I haven't had so many problems with," she says, "except that some people keep trying to call him Jerry."

Parents who've chosen less usual names talk of unanticipated problems with pronunciation and comprehension. A little girl named Leigh is sometimes called "Lay"; a child named Hannah is called Anna by some people. One of us has some regrets about calling her daughter Rory because the name is more often understood as Laurie, Corey, Tory, Dory, or even Gloria or Marie than as its rightful self.

Then there's the issue of the child's name vis à vis his or her looks and personality. Many parents wait to make a name choice until they see which of their finalists best fits the child. This makes some sense, but you should be aware that a newborn is not necessarily representative of the five- or twelve-year-old he or she will become. The chubby, noisy infant daughter you name Casey may grow into a dainty, ultrafeminine ballet dancer, while the delicate baby who seems to be the quintessential Arabella may become, ten years later, goalie on the neighborhood boys' hockey team.

This brings us to the flip side of this issue: Children can irrevocably color our perceptions of their names. You undoubtedly have unique feelings about certain names based on the children you know who bear them, and so do we. When we disagreed about whether to include a particular name on a list here, it was usually because we each knew people who brought different things to it: a handsome and irreverent Ralph, for example, vs. a boorish one; an adorable kid named Kermit vs. the frog on TV.

Reading this book can help prepare you for some of a name's eventualities, then, but not for others. You wouldn't be surprised, as our friend was, that Emily is a fashionable name or that some people are bent on using undesirable nicknames. Neither will you be unaware of both the advantages and the complications of giving your child a popular or an unusual name, or that Cameron can also be a girl's name, or that Henry has an intellectual image and so can be perceived by some people as a bit nerdy.

But no one, including you, has ultimate control over the person your child turns out to be. A name can remind you of your hopes and fears way back when childbirth was a point on the horizon, but your child—the one who's laughing or crawling or walking across the room in his own special way— can remind you that Henry by any other name, be it Michael or Melchizedek, would still be your own sweet boy.

INDEX

GIRLS' NAMES

Hadassah, 218
Hannah, 10, 54, 80, 94, 126, 150,
    151, 217, 259, 261, 271
Hanne, 238
Harmony, 195
Harper, 12
Harriet, 33, 66, 94, 110, 126, 151
Hasina, 230
Hatima, 228
Hayley, 15, 19, 54, 69, 146, 178,
    198, 242
Hazel, 33, 151
Heather, 15, 19, 45, 96, 132, 143
Hedda, 72, 221
Hedy, 242
Heidi, 103, 151, 193
Helen, 92, 93, 94, 126, 150, 151,
    261
Helena, 33, 146
Helene, 41, 146
Henrietta, 33, 66, 126, 146
Hermione, 72
Hester, 38, 151
Hil(l)ary, 15, 19, 116, 146, 178
Hilda, 151
Hinda, 228
Hogan, 27
Holland, 28
Holli, 200
Hollis, 179
Holly, 103, 146, 193, 261
Honor, 31, 94, 151
Honora, 191
Hope, 7, 31, 80, 94, 151
Hortense, 38, 151
Hyacinth, 30, 143, 157, 221, 261

Ianthe, 115
Ida, 38, 151
Ilana, 98
Iliana, 98
Ilona, 235, 242
Ilysa, 200
Ilyssa, 200
Imena, 230
Imogen, 33, 146
Imogene, 33, 146
Ina, 151
India, 28, 80, 98, 108

Indiana, 28
Inez, 151, 191
Inger, 242
Ingrid, 146, 238, 242
Iona, 66
Ione, 98
Irene, 41, 94, 151, 191
Irina, 238
Iris, 41, 147, 190
Irma, 38
Isa, 98
Isabel, 66, 98, 126, 147, 190, 221
Isabelle, 55
Isabella, 66, 98, 126, 143, 264
Isadora, 70, 98
Isobel, 239
Ivy, 30, 98, 126, 157

Jackee, 76
Jaclyn, 76
Jacqueline, 69, 108, 147, 190
Jade, 98, 108
Jael, 98, 218
Jaime, 80
Jaimie, 200
Jaleesa, 80
Jamaica, 28
Jamie, 15, 103, 153, 155, 176,
    179, 181, 194, 206
Jamila, 228
Jan, 103, 155, 178
Jane, 7, 17, 66, 115, 125, 133,
    141, 151, 221, 258, 259
Janet, 41, 94, 151, 191
Jani, 230
Janice, 41, 147, 193, 213
Janina, 237
Janine, 147
Jasmine, 30, 98, 108, 126, 147
Jayme, 200
Jayne, 76
Jazmin, 55
Jean, 41, 133, 150, 151, 179, 190,
    213, 258
Jeanette, 41, 147, 190
Jem, 75
Jemima, 31, 66, 125, 126, 218
Jen, 202
Jene, 179

Pegeen, 148, 190, 201
Peggy, 104, 189, 208
Pelline, 68
Penelope, 148
Penny, 104, 189
Pepper, 104, 130
Perry, 99, 177, 180
Persia, 28, 58
Petra, 99, 148, 234
Petrea, 68
Petronilla, 221
Petula, 73, 242
Peyton, 12
Phelan, 27
Philippa, 67, 94, 99, 148, 233
Phoebe, 58, 81, 99, 117, 127, 148,
    220, 221
Phoenix, 195
Phylicia, 76
Phyllis, 40, 42, 152, 190
Pia, 148
Piedad, 49
Pilar, 58, 99, 148, 240
Piper, 71, 104
Pippa, 104
Pola, 242
Polly, 19, 117, 127, 148, 189, 199,
    208
Pollyanna, 75
Pomeline, 68
Poppy, 30, 104, 130
Porter, 12, 26, 180
Portia, 99
Portland, 28
Posey, 30
Price, 12, 35
Primrose, 68
Priscilla, 19, 35, 143, 221
Presley, 58
Prosper, 35
Prudence, 31, 94, 152

Quinlan, 27
Quinn, 19, 27, 153
Quintana, 99, 148
Quintina, 35, 99, 148

Rachel, 16, 20, 45, 59, 95, 152,
    197, 199, 213, 217, 263

Rae, 155, 180
Raffaela, 99, 142, 143
Rain, 115, 195
Rainbow, 195, 196
Ramona, 59, 148
Randi, 104, 155, 213
Randy, 155, 180
Raquel, 71, 108
Rashida, 230
Rasia, 237
Raven, 115
Ray, 153, 180
Rayna, 20
Rebecca, 59, 95, 141, 148, 197,
    199, 217
Rebel, 195
Redmond, 27
Reed, 11, 12, 180
Regan, 19, 27, 180, 201
Reggie, 153
Regina, 42, 148, 221
Reine, 99
Renata, 99, 148, 236
Renée, 42, 148, 192, 202,
    213
Rhea, 92, 148
Rhiannon, 68, 240
Rhoda, 38, 40, 42, 152, 213
Rhonda, 38
Rhonwen, 240
Ria, 99
Ricki, 104, 155, 194, 206,
    213
Ricky, 155, 177, 179, 194
Rida, 228
Rihana, 228
Riley, 27
Rita, 42, 108, 148, 221
River, 195
Robena, 239
Roberta, 42, 152, 192, 262
Robin, 155, 178, 193
Rochelle, 148, 190, 213
Rory, 104, 155, 180, 258, 259,
    262, 271
Rosa, 148
Rosalia, 221
Rosalie, 42, 148
Rosalind, 34, 95, 148

BOYS' NAMES

Eustace, 223
Evan, 112, 117, 166, 179, 241
Evander, 172
Evelyn, 178
Everett, 166
Ezekiel, 36, 218
Ezra, 20, 36, 100, 166, 218

Fabian, 49, 166, 220, 223
Fallon, 26
Fario, 229
Farley, 171
Farrell, 12, 26
Federico, 240
Felix, 34, 75, 127, 223, 260
Ferdinand, 75, 171, 223
Fergie, 6
Fergus, 36, 223
Fidel, 129
Finn, 27, 239
Finnian, 27
Flanagan, 27
Flannery, 27
Flavian, 223
Fletcher, 233
Flint, 77, 104, 113, 139, 161, 172
Flip, 130
Florian, 223
Floyd, 34, 171
Flynn, 27
Forbes, 35
Ford, 161
Forest, 195
Forrest, 112, 166
Fortune, 35
Foster, 166
Fran, 172
Francis, 127, 171, 179
Frank, 10, 163, 191
Franklin, 38, 95, 189
Frasier, 77
Frazer, 112
Fred, 10, 162
Frederick, 8, 66, 139, 163, 164, 253
Fredric, 76
Free, 195
Frisco, 80

Gabriel, 100, 112, 117, 166, 218
Gaines, 35
Gale, 171, 172, 178
Gannon, 27
Gareth, 241
Garfield, 75
Garrett, 166, 202
Garrick, 65
Garson, 100
Gary, 6, 20, 40, 42, 68, 174, 180, 193
Gaston, 54
Gavin, 112, 239
Gaylord, 171, 172
Gaynor, 35
Gene, 179
Geoffrey, 201
George, 8, 21, 163, 180, 191, 263
Gerald, 42, 163, 192, 262
Gerard, 42, 223
Gerry, 179, 262, 263
Gershom, 218
Gerson, 218
Gideon, 36, 100, 112, 166, 216, 218
Gilad, 216
Gilbert, 42, 95, 223
Giles, 25, 223
Giorgio, 237
Glenn, 42, 174, 180
Godfrey, 34, 223
Goliath, 129
Gomer, 38, 75, 171
Gordon, 11, 95, 163
Gore, 72
Gower, 72
Grady, 27
Graham, 25, 166, 239
Grant, 35, 112
Gray, 20, 32, 65, 100, 113, 166
Greg, 174
Gregorio, 237
Gregory, 64, 112, 117, 166, 193, 198, 199, 223
Grey, 100, 166
Griffin, 27, 112, 117, 166
Griffith, 241
Grigory, 238
Grover, 75

ABOUT THE AUTHORS

LINDA ROSENKRANTZ is the author of the novel *Talk* and co-author of *Gone Hollywood* and *SoHo*. The former editor of *Auction* magazine, she now writes a nationally syndicated column on collectibles. She currently lives in Los Angeles with her husband and daughter.

PAMELA REDMOND SATRAN, former fashion features editor of *Glamour*, writes a syndicated column aimed at working parents. Her freelance articles have appeared in numerous publications, including *Self, Elle, Working Mother,* and *The Washington Post.* She lives with her husband, daughter, and son in London.

Together, the authors are at work on a series of books on British names, Irish names, and Jewish names.